Modern Sports Officiating

Modern Sp⬤rts Officiating

A Practical
Guide

by
WILLIAM A. THOMPSON
Long Beach City College,
Long Beach, California

and

RICHARD CLEGG
State University College,
New Paltz, New York

WM. C. BROWN COMPANY PUBLISHERS
Dubuque, Iowa

PHYSICAL EDUCATION

Consulting Editor

Aileene Lockhart
Texas Woman's University

HEALTH

Consulting Editor

Robert Kaplan
The Ohio State University

PARKS AND RECREATION

Consulting Editor

David Gray
California State University, Long Beach

Copyright ©1974 by Wm. C. Brown Company Publishers

Library of Congress Catalog Card Number: 73—82908

ISBN 0—697—07119—7

Printed in the United States of America

Contents

Preface

Organized athletics has enjoyed a decade of progress. But has the art of sports officiating kept pace? An obvious weakness in the preparation of sports officials is the lack of contemporary publications on the subject. *Modern Sports Officiating* is an attempt to bridge this gap.

This *practical guide* is designed for college courses in sports officiating, supervisors of sports in schools, community recreation programs and individuals preparing to enter the sports officiating field. This book aspires to provide special direction for physical education and recreation major students and prospective coaches.

It was not the desire of the authors to present the comprehensive rules and mechanics of each sport. The reader is referred to the National Federation Athletic Association and National Collegiate Athletic Association instructional literature.

Chapter One serves as an introduction to sports officiating. Special emphasis is given to the development of a sound philosophy of sports officiating, a consideration of the personal requirements of an official and a discussion of officiating as the third dimension of athletics. Chapter Two presents advice for the beginning official. Chapters Three through Ten deal specifically with the sports—baseball, basketball, football, swimming, track, volleyball, water polo and wrestling. The format for Chapters Three through Ten contains sections on the game, officials and their responsibilities, mechanics, fundamental skills, basic penalties and rulings, problem calls, official evaluations and miscellaneous considerations. Chapters One, Two, Three and Eight were the primary responsibility of Richard Clegg. Chapters Four, Five, Six, Seven, Nine and Ten and final editing were the responsibility of William A. Thompson.

In writing this book, the opinions of selected coaches and officials were sought by means of survey. Their opinions have been presented in the evaluation portion of the format. A draft of the manuscript was then submitted to a number of experienced coaches and officials for review and criticism. Thus this book is the result of the cooperative effort of many persons. The authors wish to acknowledge their indebtedness to all those who assisted in the preparation of this book.

William A. Thompson
Richard Clegg

Chapter I

Officiating
Requirements

Welcome to the challenging but rewarding job of sports officiating. If you love sports and are willing to work, you can develop a skill which is personally satisfying and beneficial to the American sports scene. There are no shortcuts to true officiating success any more than there are to true athletic success. An enthusiastic effort on your part can lead to a stimulating addition to your life.

THE OFFICIATING SCENE TODAY

The continuous and phenomenal growth of sports programs in this country has produced a great need for qualified sports officials. There is virtually no ceiling to the prospects for advancement of officials who are gifted and eager to learn. Athletic coaches and administrators at all levels of competition are constantly seeking competent officials. Coaches and administrators know that good officiating helps to produce a healthy and sportsmanlike environment and a fair determination of the winner. They wish to hire officials who will be advantageous to the sports arena. The same coaches and administrators know, on the other hand, that poorly trained, incompetent sports officials can create tensions and generate frustration among players, coaches and spectators, sometimes with serious consequences. They prefer not to hire these officials.

To put it simply, the official is the essential *third dimension* of an athletic contest. The player, the coach and the official interact, and depending upon their abilities and attitudes, combine to produce a variety of possible results—not merely a winner and a loser, but also satisfaction or disappointment, thrills or mediocrity, healthy competition or antago-

1

nism, mutual respect or mistrust. Any sports expert will acknowledge the significance of this *third dimension* to the quality of athletic competition.

The challenge of the prospective official is to develop his capabilities so that he can do what he is expected to do, regardless of the difficulties presented. Achieving a high degree of competence is chiefly the result of concentrated study and game experience in a given sport, supplemented by continuous evaluation and continuous efforts to improve.

Officiating is not a simple or easy avocation. It is a challenging task. New officials should prepare themselves thoroughly if they contemplate a continuing career in officiating. By the same token, a new official would be mistaken if he were to enter into officiating casually or for the sole purpose of financial gain. Officials should dedicate themselves toward significant goals if they expect to be successful.

Our purpose in this chapter is to establish a clear and comprehensive concept of sports officiating. The reader's goal is to develop an intelligent, realistic understanding of what competent sports officiating is and what it demands. Consider the following questions:

1. What is the fundamental aim of sports officiating?
2. What are the essential ingredients for effective sports officiating?
3. What qualities must a competent sports official possess?
4. What are the various roles which must be played while officiating?

THE FUNDAMENTAL AIM: TO CAUSE THE GAME TO PROGRESS SMOOTHLY WITHIN THE RULES

The official's overriding goal is to promote the normal progress of a contest, as it was meant to be contested, with as little interference as possible. That is *not* to say that rule enforcement should be neglected to the slightest degree, but that the competent official should not only be concerned about penalizing rule infractions; *preventing* rule infractions before they occur is also an important concern. Infractions can be prevented in two general ways: (1) by establishing a subtle but unquestioned influence over the game; and (2) by actively preventing specific infractions.

A contest frequently and unnecessarily interrupted by the official's whistle leaves no one satisfied. Under such circumstances, the official rather than the players becomes the dominant factor. Players and coaches alike respect the official who, within the playing rules, provides for continuous and uninterrupted action.

Establishing a Subtle Influence

In almost all cases, players wish to avoid rule infractions because penalties hurt. Players, especially well-trained players, will avoid many rule violations when they have cause to avoid them. The competent official capitalizes on the desires and abilities of the players by establishing his influence over the contest *early in the contest.*

In order to accomplish this, the effective sports official must be completely "warmed up" on the first play of the game in order to make *any* necessary ruling without hesitation. He realizes that the quality of "early control" established, or not established, can influence the entire game. When the official's influence is felt from the start, the game progresses as it was meant to progress. Two important ways in which you as an official can establish this influence are:

1. By *being in a position* to call the play at all times so that the players are constantly aware of your presence.
2. By *reacting immediately* to rule infractions, especially early in the contest.

When opponents, *on their own,* try to compete in accordance with the spirit and letter of the rules, the result is satisfying and rewarding to all concerned. Such a situation is not always found in athletic competition, but the dedicated official constantly seeks it. Athletics benefits from officials' efforts to produce this type of competitive environment.

Active Prevention

Obviously, more than just a subtle influence is needed occasionally in athletic competition. On these occasions the usual result is a decision by the official and the enforcement of the prescribed penalty. On other occasions, however, it is appropriate and advisable for the official to anticipate the impending infraction and to "talk the athletes out of" committing it. Direct action can and should be preventive as well as curative.

Considerable experience and background in the particular sport are necessary in order to know when and when not to issue warnings. There are moments in all sports and at all levels of play, when this type of preventive officiating can be accomplished appropriately and unobtrusively. Here are a few examples:

1. In football the head linesman cautions a lineman because he has been lining up in a position very close to "offsides"; the umpire cautions offensive linemen to "keep your hands in" as the linemen approach the scrimmage line.
2. In basketball post play, the leading official warns opposing centers to "watch your hands" in order to prevent pushing for position; before free throws the trailing official issues explicit warnings to "watch the lines."

3. In baseball, the plate umpire warns the batter about stepping out of the batter's box; while dusting off the pitcher's plate, the base umpire informs the pitcher with a "near-balk move" just what balk he is in danger of committing.
4. In track, the starter forewarns sprinters to avoid "rolling starts"; the relay lane judges show the exchange men the exact areas wherein the baton must be passed.

Such warnings not only eliminate unnecessary and unwanted infractions but they also help to establish a positive player-official relationship.

To repeat, the primary aim of the competent official is to cause the game to progress smoothly and with as little interference as possible. Preventive officiating is superior to "whistle-happy" officiating but *does not* remove the responsibility for unhesitatingly enforcing the rules.

THE ESSENTIAL INGREDIENTS

Regardless of the sport in which you are interested, four fundamental requirements must be met if you wish to be considered a successful official:

1. You must enforce the rules intelligently.
2. You must show integrity, being fair to both sides.
3. You must build sound human relations.
4. You must show primary concern for the individual athlete.

Intelligent Rule Enforcement

The rules of American sports have evolved from the concentrated attention of many experts over a period of many years. As such, the rules *command respect and demand enforcement.* The players are not adequate or appropriate rule enforcers. Rule enforcement is the job of the official; this is why he is there. He is expected to show his respect for the sport and for the players by *knowing* the rules and *enforcing* them. To do otherwise usually brings the unwanted consequences of disorganized games, unsportsmanlike acts and even the danger of injury.

Applying the rules requires the use of judgment on the part of the master official. In particular instances he will refuse to call certain apparent violations while, in other instances, he will immediately whistle down almost invisible acts. He is concerned about preserving the ideal of the sport through his rule enforcement.

Judgment by the official in applying the rules is commonly based upon the wisdom of Oswald Tower, former member of the basketball National Rules Committee. Tower said, in effect, that the purpose of the playing rules is to penalize a player who, by reason of an illegal act, places his opponent at a disadvantage. Thus, in rulings where judgment is permissible, the competent official is more concerned about the effect of an illegal act than about the act itself. For example, the slightest push of a shooter in basketball can affect his shot; if it does, an infraction has occurred and should be so ruled. There are many other examples, some of which are specified in subsequent chapters.

Authorities agree that the Tower philosophy is essentially correct, because when properly employed, it assures that the spirit of the game prevails rather than exact or petty rule enforcement. Two cautions should be noted:

1. The philosophy does not apply to all rules or even to most rules. A player is in bounds or out of bounds, a swimmer did touch or did not touch, the throw did or did not beat the base runner on a force play at second base, and so forth. In most cases, the official is asked, not to exercise his judgment, but *to call immediately what he has seen.*
2. When the philosophy *does* apply, the official must know and understand the correct rule interpretation so that his decisions are as consistent as possible. The philosophy permits the official to be flexible—if he is inconsistent as well as flexible, both he and the game will soon be in trouble.

The concept of consistency leads us to the second essential ingredient of effective sports officiating.

Absolute Integrity

The capable official wants to see the game progress correctly, without bias or inconsistency. In spite of pressures he will not be unduly influenced by the score, the time remaining, or the reactions of the players, coaches or spectators, nor will he be influenced by the direction of previous decisions. To a considerable degree, he sees each movement of the competition as a moment in itself, unconnected with what has happened previously.

In certain instances, great courage and personal confidence are required in order for an official to rule with absolute integrity, but this is exactly what he *must* do. Not even the home coach appreciates a "homer" official. Regardless of the circumstances, the sports official must be completely honest in all phases of his job, especially in his application of the rules, and also in his relationships with fellow officials, players and coaches.

Personal integrity can also be shown by what officiating assignments you *do not accept.* An official should never accept an assignment where he places himself in a compromising position. He should not work a contest when he has a close relationship with the involved schools, players or coaches. Those who hire officials actively avoid making such assignments, but in many instances only the official is able to sense a potentially compromising assignment.

Personal integrity can be shown by your relationship with officiating associations, coaches and players. Generally, these relationships should be businesslike—not political. So-called "preferred assignments" will eventually come to the gifted official, regardless of political maneuverings. The official who is not gifted is merely baiting his own trap when he attains assignments for which he is not qualified. Unfortunately, large officiating associations, by virtue of the official's anonymity, frequently create the impression that influence is more important than ability. Ultimately, such an impression is false.

Finally, personal integrity can be shown by your reliability in meeting all accepted assignments and meeting them on time. The only officiating "sin" more serious than appearing late is not appearing at all.

In retrospect, officiating integrity is a product of personal honesty and reliability. A potentially outstanding official can rise or fall according to the integrity he demonstrates.

Sound Human Relations

It has been said with considerable truth that officiating is more like an art than a science. Building sound relationships with fellow officials, players, coaches and spectators while under the fire of intense athletic rivalry calls for "an artist's touch."

Relationship with fellow officials.   For the most part, officials are on their own at the contest. If their mutual support and teamwork break down, problems in other relationships will certainly increase. Here are a few specific suggestions which may clarify what is needed in order to produce real teamwork among officials:

1. *Always* arrive early enough to consult with your fellow officials before the game so that you can agree on mechanics and rule interpretations and begin to become acquainted with one another.
2. *Never* argue with a fellow official.
3. Agree in advance about who will call what (and who will not call what).
4. Agree in advance about how you may assist one another in making decisions which require assistance.
5. Decide in advance the circumstances, if any exist, whereupon one official may overrule or cancel the decision of another. This prac-

tice is permissible in a few sports—although it is to be avoided. Nonetheless, such a touchy issue should be agreed upon in advance.

6. During the contest, avoid the temptation to explain your fellow official's decision. Let him make his own explanations and then back him up.

7. The more experienced officials should take the initiative to help inexperienced officials. Such assistance can be appropriate and useful *before* and *after* the contest, but seldom *during* the contest.

Relationships with players. Good relationships between players and officials are of fundamental importance to effective officiating. Coaches and spectators can sense the quality of the player-official relationship, and their judgment of the official is influenced by what they sense. Officials should be neither overly friendly nor aloof in their dealings with players. Players tend to mistrust an official who seems to be trying to win a popularity contest with both teams. They expect an official to act like an *official* who has an important job to do.

The degree to which an official should try to be helpful varies considerably according to the sport and the level of play. In professional sports a particularly helpful official would be treated with amazement, amusement or scorn; whereas, in youth contests a competent official will not hesitate to actually teach the rules at appropriate moments.

A domineering or dictatorial official upsets the players. Officials must be or at least act humane and approachable. An official must show respect for the players if he wishes to gain respect. Hustle and enthusiasm also increase player respect.

When unsportsmanlike acts occur, whether directly involving the official or not, these acts should be penalized immediately, but in as calm a manner as possible. Unsportsmanlike acts usually create excitement and emotional reactions by players, coaches and spectators alike. What is especially needed under such circumstances is not anger or revenge but an accurate and efficient penalty enforced confidently and calmly.

Relationships with coaches. As implied by the rules of most sports, contact between the coaches and officials should be businesslike, friendly, respectful and *limited.* The coach is concerned about an official's mechanics and judgment. He is not likely to be concerned about whether or not an official wishes to be his friend. Occasionally, coaches become extremely upset with officials. Under such circumstances, considerable tact is needed. Often the upset coach is the type that can be calmed down almost as easily as he became excited. A businesslike, but not unfriendly explanation of the decision may prevent serious consequences.

The official should not overreact to the excited coach, but he must enforce obvious infractions by the coach. If there is a choice between protecting the coach or the game, the game must be considered first.

Relationships with spectators. While the official's main attention is directed to the game and the players and partially to the coaches, the presence of spectators cannot be ignored. The trend of an athletic event can be harmed by intense spectator reactions. However, this rarely occurs if the officials of the game do their work well; that is, if they maintain good position, are decisive in judgment and signal clearly.

In summary, sound public relations must be a part of competent officiating because sports involve human beings with opposing loyalties. These human beings possess different backgrounds, abilities and emotional responses. In fact some of them will not like officials. Apparently the sports official cannot satisfy everyone, nor should this be his aim. He should show respect for others, avoid antagonizing anyone, and be approachable. His main efforts should be directed toward the best officiating job he can produce. When, in part because of high-quality officiating, the contest is played skillfully and fairly, the basis for common goodwill has been established.

Your Foremost Concern: The Individual Athlete

The master official is primarily concerned with the protection of the players. In most instances his actions are prompted by this concern. For example:

1. He wants to prevent injuries, and he knows that in many sports good officiating can prevent many damaging and unnecessary injuries.
2. He wants to encourage sportsmanlike behavior, and he understands the importance of his job in promoting such behavior.
3. He knows that correct rulings can motivate player improvement through the trial-and-error learning process.
4. He does not discourage questions on the rules, because he knows that players don't know all the rules.
5. He wants to keep all the players in the game, and he knows that in many cases the ejection or disqualification of a player can be prevented.
6. He is willing to eject or disqualify a player when the rules and spirit of the game demand such action because the protection of other players and the quality of the game itself are involved. In addition, the particular player can learn from the experience of being disqualified.

The official who is able and willing to use "protection of the players" as his guide will be amazed at its effectiveness, especially in making difficult decisions. To test this theory, try it against any seemingly hopeless officiating situation that you can imagine. In this imaginary situation, ask yourself, what should be done for the players' protection? Perhaps the indicated decision will not be completely acceptable, but it will be the *best* decision if it is based upon concern for the individual athlete. The beginning official must be constantly reminded of his responsibility to the players.

QUALITIES OF A COMPETENT OFFICIAL

If one hundred different sports officiating experts submitted their own lists of essential qualifications of a master official, one might expect one hundred different listings. If asked to place a given set of qualifications in order of their importance, the same experts might again be expected to differ in their opinions. Thus, the qualities selected by the authors and the following list bear no claim of infallibility or even comprehensiveness. Nevertheless, such a list of qualities is meant to clarify the game-by-game requirements of successful sports officiating.

The following list was derived from survey and interview responses from scores of recognized officials and coaches, in addition to the personal experiences of the authors. The purposes of the list are (1) to specify the requirements of effective officiating; (2) to guide and motivate improvement; and (3) to establish guidelines for the evaluation of officials (either self-evaluation or evaluation by those who hire officials). Good eyesight was not included, although its importance cannot be questioned.

I. Precise Knowledge of Playing Rules

The rules of any game provide the direction for play. Officials are expected to see that the game is played according to those rules. Mastery of game rules is a continuing effort. Early in the preparation stages prospective officials study rule case books and discuss rules in detail in the officiating association class meetings. The most effective means of resolving confusion and promoting understanding in complex sections of the rules is accomplished in smaller study groups. Competent officials make it a practice to review the total rule book the night before an assignment. The official finds it helpful to analyze carefully difficult sections of the rules on the day of the game. Following the game, officials should critique their individual effort and the performance of the officiating unit. This will allow for immediate attention to deficiencies in the understanding of the rules while situations are still fresh in the mind. Finally, officiating associations in many areas of the country meet socially during the off-season in an effort to keep their officials posted on rule changes for the coming season.

II. Judgment

Judgment in an individual contest should be based primarily upon a thorough knowledge and understanding of the playing rules. No official ever has said or probably ever will be able to say, "My judgment is complete and perfect." Development of good judgment is a never-ending process. The official who *continues* to study the rules and to apply his officiating experiences to personal improvement is the official who will succeed. Good judgment is a foremost qualification of the top-notch official, because it permits him to make the correct decision unhesitatingly under any game circumstances. It also develops the respect and approval of players and coaches alike.

When an official is able to make one sound decision after another, his control of the game becomes evident. The game progresses as it was meant to progress, with the players and the action, rather than the official, playing the dominant role.

Competitive playing or coaching experience in a given sport greatly helps the judgment of a new official, but such an experience is certainly not enough in itself.

III. Good Mechanics

Mechanics refers to the routine procedures surrounding what the official does. The two primary areas of mechanics are signaling and positioning. When more than one official is involved, "teamwork" becomes a third area of mechanics, wherein additional signaling and positioning responsibilities are necessary. Signals may be made by mechanical device, by voice or gesture, depending upon the sport or the circumstance. The mechanics of positioning, signaling and teamwork are all of essential importance to a professional performance. Good positioning is necessary if you are to see what you are supposed to see. Sharp, unhesitating and unhurried signals are necessary to communicate your decisions and to build the confidence of everyone regarding your officiating ability. Commonly recognized teamwork procedures are necessary to ensure to the greatest possible extent that (1) every conceivable action is covered and ruled upon and (2) disagreement is eliminated or minimized.

When proper mechanics are performed precisely, the game progresses without confusion or unnecessary delay. There is nothing complicated or magical about the mechanics of any sport. Good mechanics are not too difficult to develop *if* correct habits are established early in the official's career. Difficulty does occur when the new official unsuspecting-ly forms incorrect habits. Mechanics, good or bad, are habitual actions. It is much easier to learn the correct habit first than to unlearn an incorrect habit later.

Like playing rules, mechanics have evolved from the efforts of many people for many years and, therefore, they should command the respect and acceptance of new officials. The first two obligations of a new official are to learn the playing rules and to develop correct habits of mechanics.

IV. Hustle

By the colloquial definition, hustle means to move or act with reso-lute energy. With the possible exception of good judgment, no quality commands more respect and approval than hustle. Hustle is highly valued on the athletic scene by all concerned including fellow officials. It is that quality which improves athletes most, which coaches wish most to teach and which is greatly admired and respected by spectators, coaches and athletes alike.

Depending on the particular sport, hustle can be demonstrated in several different ways. It should be defined broadly to include such re-lated attributes as *alertness, physical effort, dedication* and *enthusiasm.* Hustle—or the lack of it—*is apparent,* regardless of the sport you happen to be officiating. A hustling official will display better mechanics, see more and enjoy his work more. The opposites are true of the official who is lazy or uninterested. As one dimension of the sports scene, the official is expected to demonstrate this valued attribute. But whether hustle is expected or not, the hustling official will certainly do a better job. Coaches continually rank hustle high on their list of positive officiating attributes.

V. Decisiveness

The decisive official converts a controversial or judgmental decision into an accepted-ruling decision merely by his decisiveness. The usual result is a continuous contest apparently decided by the skills of the players, not an interrupted game "unfairly" affected by the "questionable" decisions of an official. The experienced, competent official realizes that his judgment is not subject to formal protest in any case; he, therefore, avoids any *unnecessary* and *hopeless* controversy by ruling decisively on close decisions; *the closer the decision, the greater the decisiveness.* Com-pare these examples with your personal experience.

1. In football, the sideline official (head linesman or field judge) should signal immediately whether or not a touchdown has been scored when the ball carrier is close to the goal line.

2. In basketball, the trailing official should cancel the potential basket immediately and decisively when the period ends just before the "try" was in flight.
3. In baseball, the "bang-bang" play at first base should be resolved by a definite and demonstrative gesture; on the other hand, the obvious decision requires but a minimal gesture.
4. In wrestling, a fall which is very close to being merely a near-fall should be accompanied by a much more decisive signal than the obvious fall.

When there is a hesitant, indecisive, delayed decision, one opponent or the other is sure to believe that the decision was incorrect. Since a decision must be made in any event, the competent official makes all his decisions decisively.

VI. Poise

Athletic contests are exciting and, therefore, frequently arouse the emotions of the participants and spectators. Contests can get out of hand when emotions run high. Officials cannot control the emotions of others, but they are expected to control their own and to show poise, regardless of the circumstances.

Confidence and calmness are the basic components needed. Persons who lack personal confidence or who are excitable or emotional do not usually make good officials. Such persons add to existing tensions by overreacting in pressurized moments. On the other hand, the poised official contributes to a controlled atmosphere. During tense moments, he acts deliberately, almost slowly, whenever possible. The greater the momentary tension, the greater is the need for calmness (e.g., removing the player from a contest for unsportsmanlike conduct). Obviously, to maintain poise under extreme tension is not easy. To do so under certain circumstances requires nearly superhuman personal control. Most outstanding officials have developed the habit, consciously or unconsciously, of *acting* calmly at times when, in fact, they are very excited.

Athletic contests should be governed by the abilities of the players and the playing regulations, not by uncontrolled emotions. The poised sports official sometimes is the only person in the position and with the authority to return the game to the "healthy excitement" of properly supervised athletic competition.

VII. Consistency

If a count were taken of the officiating qualities most frequently criticized by and most upsetting to coaches and players, undoubtedly inconsistency would lead the list. Coaches and players expect the rules to apply equally to both teams. Even true consistency is open to misinterpretation by players, coaches and spectators, as well as by officials. True consistency results not from attempting to even up both sides but, from applying the *correct rule interpretation* to each *separate* competitive act. The underlying truth is that, especially where judgment is concerned, *no two competitive situations are exactly alike.* If an official applies accurate judgment, according to the letter and meaning of the rules, to each separate decision, he will be consistent—because the *correct rule interpretation is unchanging.* Proper judgment and interpretation are the sources of consistency. The official who understands and applies the rules and their interpretations will gain the reputation of being consistent.

VIII. Courage

This quality is closely related to objectivity and integrity. Nevertheless, no list of necessary officiating qualities could be complete without separating and emphasizing the personal courage which is necessary for effective sports officiating.

It takes a degree of courage merely to don the black and white striped shirt and report to the contest. Unfortunately, sports officials in the United States traditionally do not arouse immediate feelings of congeniality and comradeship from players, coaches, spectators and other officials. Unknown officials have to prove themselves and everyone is aware of this. The really tough decision may occur at any moment and that is just the decision that separates the superior official from the mediocre. The superior official calls them all to the best of his ability, because he has the courage to do so. He realizes that he is empowered by the rules and *obligated to the players and coaches* to make the difficult decision. He is well aware that two of the *most unfavorable* things he can do are (1) *avoid* a decision where a decision is required, or (2) *make* a decision merely because the players, coaches and/or spectators demand it.

IX. Rapport

Implications regarding rapport have already been made under the section dealing with sound relationships. Rapport refers to the quality of relating effectively to others. Good rapport with others is a desirable quality in many lines of human endeavor; its importance in sports officiating certainly cannot be denied and should not be underrated.

While conscientiously meeting the many requirements of his job, the official must not neglect human relationships. The great official can certainly show his humane and friendly nature without compromising his job; he not only can but he does. He knows that, as an official, he has enough problems without creating additional difficulties in human relationships. Each official will find his own way to build rapport with fellow officials, players, coaches and spectators. His own way should reflect his own personality.

Regardless of your individual personality, rapport can be improved if you:

1. Demonstrate courtesy and respect for coaches and players.
2. Show a sense of humor at appropriate moments.
3. Are approachable and receptive to questions.

X. Objectivity

As human beings, officials, like others, *can be* influenced by various pressures. But unlike many others, the official is *not supposed to be* influenced by external pressures. Perhaps an official's pregame preparation should include mentally pledging: "I solemnly swear to call only what I see and *not* to be swayed by what people say, by my previous calls or by personalities (including my own)."

Most officials benefit from, first, consciously recognizing their own potential for being influenced and, second, seriously attempting to improve their complete objectivity in each game. Otherwise, the temptations of a given moment in the competition can lead the normally well-meaning individual to make a popular decision rather than a correct decision.

Perhaps the plate umpire in baseball best personifies the need for objectivity. The effective plate umpire does not try to "even them up" when making close ball and strike decisions, even though he is in a perfect position to do so. Each pitch is a different pitch. Each pitch is a ball or a strike regardless of which player or team is at bat, what the score or the count is or what was called previously. The less-than-great umpire, without realizing it, is tempted to "help" a team or a player (or himself), and the result is an inconsistency which seriously harms the game; soon no one knows what to expect. The suggestion most commonly associated with sports officiating in the United States is "Call them as you see them." The fact that this phrase is not yet trite, in spite of its continued usage, indicates the importance of objectivity to sports officiating.

XI. Reaction Time

Assuming that judgment is correct, decisions which are made quickly have a greater chance of being accepted without question. An official with a slow reaction time is open to question. An official with fast reactions frequently can make his decision almost simultaneously with the moment of the infraction. Thus, his "subtle influence" on the game is quickly and firmly established. The slow reacting official frequently compensates for his slowness by developing the poor habit of "anticipating" impending infractions and consequently calling infractions that did not occur.

The extent to which reaction time can be "improved" is open to question. Experimental evidence appears to indicate (1) that different individuals have different but definite physiological limits upon the speed of their reactions or reflexes, and (2) that the speed of executing any given act can, within the individual's limits, be quickened through practice. A beginning official can expect some early quickening of his whistle, his signals or his recall gun *while he is learning the particular reaction.* Following this initial learning period, the official's speed of reactions to various situations will become stabilized within his own individual limits. It is clear, in any case, that a person with severe limits upon his basic reaction time will be wise not to become a sports official.

XII. Conditioning and Appearance

These two qualifications are closely related since both can be improved up to minimum levels. Also, they are both related to the pride and dedication of the official.

Conditioning. In several sports the quality of the officiating job can be limited by the physical condition of the official. Such is certainly the case in basketball, football, baseball and wrestling. To put it simply, good conditioning is necessary *throughout the contest* of certain sports to allow you to: (1) be where you should be; (2) maintain your alertness and good judgment; and (3) hold up your end of the teamwork with your fellow official. A tired official certainly cannot meet all the requirements for good officiating. The primary components of good officiating condition appear to be good cardiorespiratory endurance and strong legs. Most outstanding officials put themselves through a graduated conditioning program prior to the start of the season. By doing so, they can avoid early season injuries, especially torn muscles, and can produce up to expectations at their first assignment of the year. A jogging program is suggested, and would certainly enable officials, who have varying full-time jobs, to intelligently prepare themselves for the coming season.

Appearance. A certain razor company once increased its sales through the slogan: "Look sharp! Feel sharp! Be sharp!" This slogan presents excellent advice to sports officials. "Feel sharp" has implications for physical and mental preparation, especially for conditioning. "Be sharp" suggests that an official react quickly, hustle and display good judgment and mechanics. We are concerned here with "looking sharp."

Most officials' associations have minimum dress regulations which should be observed. An official who reports for duty in an unkempt, dirty uniform does not inspire the confidence of players and coaches. Such officials start the game at a disadvantage. Adequate conditioning and appearance *can* be attained. It makes no sense, nor is it justifiable, for an official to report for a game in an unfit or sloppy condition.

A review of the qualities advocated indicates the impossibility of your becoming a *perfect* official. How many officials have you observed who combine all of these qualities? The point to be made here, however, is that you or any other prospective official can improve each of the qualities. Your performance and your enjoyment of officiating will depend upon how much you improve.

THE ROLES

As the action and tempo of a contest progress and change, the official must oftentimes assume several different roles, depending upon the particular circumstances. According to the particular situation, it may be necessary for the sports official to assume partially the role of an educator, a salesman, a psychologist or a statesman. The competent official recognizes the particular need under the given circumstance and assumes the indicated role.

As an educator.   He briefly explains the rule and its proper interpretation.

As a salesman.   He influences players toward fair, clean and sportsmanlike play and away from unsportsmanlike conduct.

As a psychologist.   He understands the feelings of the players, coaches and spectators, and through his understanding he is able to show respect and in turn gain their respect.

As a statesman.   He speaks clearly and logically when it is necessary for him to speak.

SUMMARY

There is a great need for qualified sports officials to meet the demands of an expanding sports scene. Regardless of the level of competition, the benefits of athletic competition are greater when the competition is guided by capable sports officials. Such officials cause particular contests to be conducted as they were meant to be conducted and cause the result of the competition to be based upon player ability and observance of the rules.

Sports officials should be guided by an overall aim of causing the contest to progress smoothly with as little interference as possible. The essential ingredients of effective sports officiating are (1) intelligent rule enforcement, (2) absolute integrity, (3) sound human relationships, and (4) a focus upon the protection of the individual athlete.

Competent sports officials continuously attempt to improve themselves and measure their performance against standards such as the "qualities of a competent official" included in this book. They also are prepared to assume several different roles, according to the demands of the particular circumstances.

Sports officiating is a difficult but rewarding avocation. The primary awards will be related more to personal development and satisfaction than to financial gain. When sports officials are well trained, highly dedicated and more aware of the total requirements of their responsibilities, athletic competition will benefit.

Chapter II

Getting off to a
Good Start

The first few games you work can be of particular importance to your future as an official. A general pattern of relative success, adequacy, or failure becomes evident to you, and to the players and coaches for whom you work. (Obviously, the early pattern of your work can change in either direction after these early assignments.) Early success will encourage you and motivate you further to improve your knowledge, judgment, mechanics and mannerisms. Early failure or mediocrity can hamper your early development as a sports official. Premature discouragement undoubtedly is the greatest cause of a high "drop-out" rate during the first year of officiating. Much of this discouragement *can be avoided* through preparation and a keener understanding of certain pitfalls which threaten the potentially blossoming career of the inexperienced official.

Our purpose is to provide you with practical suggestions which will help you to achieve success during your early officiating assignments. *Anyone* can follow these suggestions. The only requirements are effort and interest.

PRELIMINARY PREPARATION

If you follow the suggestions within this section, you will be prepared *in a general sense* for the mental, physical and emotional realities of your first assignment.

1. *Watch as many games as you can, not as a spectator but as an official.* Whether you are watching the game in person or on television imagine yourself as being one of that game's officials.

Live the game with them. Make decisions with them (or criticize their decisions). Imagine yourself blowing the whistle, signaling, talking with the team captains, dealing with the emergencies that are a part of that game, and so forth.

It is beneficial to watch any game at any level—professional, college, high school or recreational—but the benefits are greater if you can arrange to see contests at the same level as that of your first expected assignments. The requirements at each level are somewhat different.

Try to arrive at the game in time to observe the officials during the pregame activity. Bring a notebook and approach your analysis of the officials in an organized fashion. Know in advance what you are looking for. You might organize your notes under some of the following categories.

a) What were the strengths and weaknesses of each official?

b) What happened in the game that (1) created problems or (2) caused the game to progress well from the officials' points of view?

c) Were there any particularly outstanding or particularly poor decisions or mechanics? What were they and how much did they affect the game?

d) Specifically, how well did the officials communicate, maintain good position, react decisively, know their rules and mechanics and show good judgment?

e) If you had a chance, how would you advise each official regarding his individual improvement? (Refer to the eleven qualities discussed in Chapter 1.)

In officiating any "ball" sport, perhaps the most common and the most difficult fault for the inexperienced official to correct is that of habitually focusing complete attention on the ball, to the exclusion of action away from the ball. This habit can and must be broken. It can be corrected to a considerable degree before your first assignment if you concentrate on it while watching other officials work. When you watch any game, *watch it as an official.*

2. *Participate actively in officials' meetings.* Unfortunately, many sports officials, especially the experienced officials, approach training meetings of the local officials' association apathetically. Such an approach can "rub off" onto the young, prospective official and greatly hamper his development. Regardless of the attitudes of other officials, these meetings *can be* great learning experiences if they are approached in a positive and active man-

ner. There is a wealth of knowledge and experience available to you at these meetings. You can find the answer to almost any officiating question that you have. You can gain the acquaintanceship of locally outstanding men. Strong sports officials take pride in their work and are willing, if not anxious, to assist the less experienced official.

3. *Secure adequate officiating equipment.* Until you earn a reputation as a qualified sports official, you must at least *look* the part. Avoid the shortcuts of wrong colored shoes, socks, belts and jackets. Don't use a cheap whistle. Such compromises almost certainly will return to plague you. Until you demonstrate your skill, you are only an image, an impression. You might as well present a favorable, professional image. Your first few assignments will be challenging enough in themselves without adding to the burden by *appearing to be unprepared.*

4. *Be sure that you are in adequate physical condition.* You will be amazed at how physically tiring your first games will be. The inexperienced official feels a need to overhustle. Because of his lack of experience, he runs farther than is necessary and does not know how or when to conserve his energy.

5. *Volunteer your services at preseason scrimmages.* There is no substitute for direct experience. All coaches who plan preseason competitive experiences for their teams would like some of these to be officiated. The preseason scrimmage presents an opportunity for the official, as well as the players and coaches, to tune up, to identify and correct weaknesses in advance. An added benefit is the appreciation and goodwill of coaches that you create by volunteering to help. Many new officials have found that willingness to donate their services before the season has resulted in more assignments later.

6. *Concentrate on the basics first.* You cannot "learn it all" before the first assignment. In fact, you will *never* learn it all. Too much concern over minor details early in your career bogs you down and is confusing to the learning process. For example, a new basketball official should not expect to know and demonstrate every hand signal at his first game. The "basics" for your early concentration are:

a) A knowledge of the common rules and penalties.
b) An understanding of the fundamentals of positioning mechanics.
c) The ability to use routine signals.

d) An effort to employ the fundamental aspects of teamwork with fellow officials.

PREGAME PREPARATION

This section is meant to help you feel prepared *specifically* for each of your first officiating assignments.

1. *If possible, know the teams and the playing areas.* The veteran official frequently has an added advantage over the neophyte because he has advance knowledge about the opposing teams, their coaches and the playing site. He is more mentally prepared for his job because he knows the playing styles, the coaches' mannerisms, the number and emotional involvement of spectators and characteristics of the playing area, such as space, obstacles, surface, timing device and special ground rules.

   The new man cannot possibly gather and digest all of his information but, through a bit of advance preparation, he can learn some of it. He can check local newspapers. He can ask other officials. He might even observe a game or practice session previous to his assignment.

2. *If possible, plan to travel to the game with a fellow official.* A phone call or two a few days in advance of the contest can help to produce a better officiated game. There is no end to the number of points that can be discussed by officials working together in any sport. Mutual respect and confidence can grow during the trip. A good relationship with a fellow official is especially rewarding for the inexperienced man.

3. *Plan to be at the game early.* Do not accept an assignment if you cannot expect to be there, dressed and ready, approximately one-half hour before the game's scheduled time. Estimate your travel time conservatively to prevent being late. The hurried official who runs onto the court two minutes before the center jump is asking for trouble and is creating a very bad impression.

4. *Be well rested and sharp.* Occasionally the official will find himself in the middle of a game in which one near-impossible situation after another will occur. If he is tired and dull-witted on these occasions, these "near-impossible" situations become *impossible.* Be sure that you get a good night's sleep before each assignment. Avoid large meals immediately before the game.

5. *Expect the worst.* Never anticipate an easy game. Fortunately you will have easy games from time to time, but you will enjoy

these more and *get more of them* if they come as pleasant surprises. We are not suggesting that you should be worried or fearful but that you approach each assignment with the same kind of respect and seriousness as that of a former nonswimmer approaching deep water. Your chances of meeting the challenge of a really tough game will be better.

AT THE GAME

Each individual official soon develops his own individual officiating personality and habits. Until these become apparent and are further implemented and embellished, the inexperienced official needs some guidelines which will keep him out of trouble. Here are some suggestions.

1. *Don't try to oversell yourself.* Most new officials understandably want to prove immediately to players, coaches and spectators alike that they are not only capable but friendly and even personable; however, such an impression will develop with true meaning only through the job you do. You want such an impression to prevail after the game more than before the game. If a coach does not know an official, he may mistrust one whose approach is overly cordial or personal. You must be approachable, but as an "official" in every sense of the word, you are expected to maintain *distance* from players, coaches and spectators.

   Perhaps a good way to summarize this important but rather subtle point is to suggest that you should let good, positive relationships grow naturally and without force mostly from the skill that you demonstrate and partly from your willingness to cooperate and to be approached.

2. *Actively try to avoid the common mistakes frequently made by inexperienced officials.* Awareness of these common mistakes can help you to combat them and also reassure you that most inexperienced officials do make them. Following are some of the most commonly made mistakes and suggestions on how to avoid them:

   a) *Over-anticipating.* Nothing can be called until it *happens.* It is better to be a split-second late in your decision than to rule on something that simply did not happen or that had no effect on the competition.

   b) *Rushing your signals.* The cause for this is the same as for overanticipation, that is, over-anxiousness. Tell yourself: "Don't rush, let it happen"; be deliberate, then signal in a decisive manner when you know it happened. Many rushed signals are not even seen; thus the effect of a given decision is lost or diminished.

c) *Not enforcing the rules.* As an inexperienced official, you will almost certainly approach your early assignments cautiously. It is frequently noticeable that this caution can be translated into overlooking rule infractions which "really didn't affect the game that much" but which in actuality *did* affect the game. If you are experiencing this type of difficulty, it is sometimes helpful to remind yourself that both teams and both coaches depend on you for a fair outcome of the game. A fair outcome will not be possible without courageous and honest officiating.

d) *Being out of position.* The veteran official maintains good position habitually; the new man must compensate for his lack of habits by mentally anticipating the flow of action. It is helpful to remind yourself constantly during "dead spots" of the game about the basic positioning mechanics found in any sport. In basketball, for example, just before the jump ball, the outside man can anticipate two or three possible movements depending upon the outcome of the jump.

e) *Overreacting to complaints.* Remind yourself that no matter how hard you work, or even how competently you perform, complaints will come to all officials in all sports. Your reaction to "beefs" early in your career will be of great importance to your development. Even when you *know* your decision was correct, react to the complaints with calmness and firmness. If the complaint regards your judgment, nothing can be done about it. If, on the other hand, a rule interpretation is involved and you are not certain about the rule, you might wish to confer quickly with a fellow official. Incorrect rule interpretations can and should be reversed.

Perhaps the most difficult circumstance for a new official is a confrontation with a coach who habitually baits officials. If such a coach decides that you have "rabbit ears," you will soon be in serious trouble. Under such circumstances, try to think of the game and the players—not of the coach or of yourself. Disregard the first taunts. If they continue, approach the coach *inconspicuously* and *positively*, not in anger. You will be helping the game, the players and yourself (not to mention the coach himself) if you can settle him down.

f) *Showing your nervousness.* Experience is the best cure for nervousness, but even the totally inexperienced official can use his human talents to combat his undesirable nervousness. Constantly talk yourself into *being deliberate,* not rushing. Be an actor. Even though you may be quite unsure of yourself, you don't have to *show* your lack of confidence. Actively *fake* a confident manner. Play the role of the most poised official that you have ever seen. If you really throw yourself into this type of role-playing, you will be amazed at the results.

AFTER THE GAME

Certain procedures following each early assignment can guarantee improvement. These procedures are commonly overlooked by new officials. The idea is simple: "Be sure that you complete the learning process of each early assignment."

1. *After the game discuss it with fellow officials.* The other officials have seen you in action, they know what kind of a game it was, and they know something about officiating. Ask them for suggestions. Preferably, take notes on what they tell you.

2. *Keep your own "book" on your personal improvement.* As soon as possible after each early assignment, write down every significant fact that you can remember. Evaluate not only your performance but that of the other officials. You can learn from their strengths and weaknesses as well as from your own. Your book might include some of the following sections:
   a) New rule interpretations that you learned.
   b) New mechanics techniques that you observed in the other officials.
   c) Your identifiable weaknesses (rules and mechanics) in this particular game.
   d) Questions to ask at the next officials' meeting.
   e) Specific goals for improving the next assigned game.

   Many of the best and most experienced professional and college sports officials keep such a notebook because they know that there is always room for improvement. Certainly the values to an inexperienced man of such an organized approach are greater.

Hard work and intelligent preparation guarantee relative success for every athlete. The same is true for sports officials. Just as a college freshman basketball player would, you also should set high standards regarding preparation for your first sports officiating season.

Good luck!

Chapter III

Baseball

THE GAME

While players need to throw, catch, bat, bunt, field and know countless strategical situations, umpires also need to prepare themselves specifically for a *multitude of situations* that will test their skill. In the first few baseball games that he umpires, the beginning umpire will quickly learn that this is a unique game, which imposes unique demands on its officials.

First, he will learn that the baseball umpire, especially the plate umpire, is more completely *alone* and *on his own* than is any other official in any other sport. This means that he must possess a high level of *personal confidence* in his ability as an umpire. He makes the decision, an isolated decision, and he must live with it and make it stand with little or no backing from anyone else, including his fellow umpires.

Second, he will learn that to argue with, to bait and even ridicule a baseball official is commonplace and traditional to the game. Despite efforts to restrict or eliminate such signs of disrespect, they remain a "part of the game," a reality that each baseball official must learn to tolerate, *yet permit only so far and no farther*. This means that the baseball official must possess *patience* and must *understand* the game, its players and coaches.

The third challenge involves the extensive and precise rules of baseball and the need for continuous study. To an amazing degree, almost every freak play that ever has happened or could happen is covered in the rules. There is no substitute for knowing the rules.

Fourth, almost every baseball game produces several very close ball-or-strike and safe-or-out decisions. The umpire must possess *finely tuned eyesight* and *fast reactions* in order to rule immediately and decisively.

Fifth, the umpire, as well as the spectator, will often find the pace of a baseball game to be hypnotically slow. The effect of such a pace, especially on the base umpire, can lull him to sleep. *Steady concentration* is a must for the effective umpire. The better umpires frequently ask themselves during a game, "What could happen next?" in order to maintain their alertness. Also, due to the pace of the game, both *physical* and *mental endurance* is required. The umpire is expected to rule just as effectively in the ninth inning as in the first inning.

Finally, baseball is one game that does not progress according to the clock. It is a seven, nine or extra inning game which could last an hour and a half or *four* hours and a half.

OFFICIALS AND THEIR RESPONSIBILITIES

The officials of baseball include the umpires and the scorer. From one to six umpires may officiate baseball games, depending on the level of play. The vast majority of games, however, are officiated by just two umpires: the *plate umpire* (or the umpire-in-chief) and the *base umpire* (or field umpire). The major emphasis in this chapter is on the two umpire system.

Plate Umpire

The umpire-in-chief takes a position behind the catcher and renders decisions on balls and strikes and almost all fair and foul batted balls. He has general responsibility for the conduct of the game, establishes, as is necessary, special "ground" rules or other regulations, informs the official scorer of changes in the lineups, and has the sole authority to forfeit the game. The plate umpire is constantly making decisions, an estimated 200 to 250 pitches per game, among others. The plate umpire runs the game and sets the tempo. In almost all cases, the plate umpire is paid more than the base umpire—and for good reason.

Base Umpire

The base umpire varies his field position according to the game situation and makes almost all of the decisions at the three bases and in the outfield. He has equal responsibility with the plate umpire for all rulings, including discipline and control, with the exception of those specified for the plate umpire. The base umpire covers a large territory while the decisions he renders are fewer and more irregular. He tends to be in the background more than the plate umpire.

Umpires

Each umpire may rule on any matter not specifically covered in the rules. Each may disqualify any coach, player or substitute and banish any other person from the playing field. One umpire may seek the assistance of another umpire on any decision, but under no circumstances may any umpire seek to reverse the decision of a fellow umpire. Umpires are encouraged to work both as plate and base umpires to enhance their opportunity for advancement. A degree of personal flexibility is necessary to adapt to either responsibility, since the responsibilities of each are so different.

Official Scorer

The official scorer operates semi-independently of the umpires. Normally, his only contact with them occurs when there are lineup changes or questions concerning the scoring of a run or the number of outs. In certain lower levels of baseball, the scorer is required to report immediately to the plate umpire a player batting out of turn, in order to alleviate technicality rulings.

MECHANICS

Mechanics is defined as the standard operating procedure for officials working a game. In baseball officiating mechanics, voice and hand signals are minimal and relatively uncomplicated. The major attention must be devoted to *positioning* mechanics, especially by the field umpire, and teamwork mechanics. When one considers the problems imposed on umpires by distance and speed of action, he understands immediately why position and teamwork need emphasis. The focus again will be on the two man system, the plate umpire and the base umpire.

Positioning

The difference between a called ball and a called strike can be as slight as you wish to imagine: an inch, a quarter of an inch or a sixteenth of an inch. In order to reduce his margin of error, it is necessary for the *plate umpire* to secure and maintain a position where he is low, he is close to the catcher and, most important, his view of the pitch remains unobstructed by the catcher and the batter. The plate umpire should learn to glide slightly with each pitch. He should *stay with* the pitch and avoid the natural tendency to "back off" or to "raise up" as the pitch arrives. The natural tendency to "blink," especially when the batter swings, can be reduced through practice.

Generally, there are two recommended plate umpire positions: the National League (inside corner) position and the American League (over the top) position. The prospective umpire should experiment with each before making his personal selection. Then he should strive for improvement in technique relative to different types of pitchers, catchers and hitters. The prospective umpire will find that it is easier to umpire from the inside corner (that side edge of the plate closest to the hitter) with an inside chest protector than with a "balloon" type protector. He will find that the inside corner position permits a closer view of the total strike zone and of the inside corner and low pitches, but that the over-the-top position permits more flexibility in moving with the pitch as it approaches the strike zone and more accuracy in calling the "high strike" and the outside corner.

It should be emphasized from the outset that *base umpire* starting positions can be varied somewhat according to the situation and the

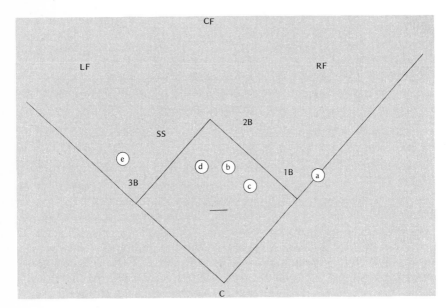

FIG. 3.1

Base Umpire Starting Positions in the Two-Umpire System (before the Pitch):

a — No base runners
b — Runner on first
c — Optional position, runner on first
d — Runner on second, first and second, first and third, or bases loaded
e — Runner on third, infield in

preference of individual umpires. It is important that, before each pitch, the umpire place himself in a position that will enable him to feel as comfortable, ready and confident as possible. Figure 3.1 clearly illustrates the three basic starting positions and several alternative positions for the base umpire.

The Mechanics on Specific Calls of the Base Umpire

Batted ball to the outfield. On any batted ball to the outfield (with few exceptions) the field umpire wants to be inside the base lines as quickly as possible. This will shorten the distance he must run to allow himself a view of both the ball and the runner. He should attempt to maintain a slight lead on the batter-runner so that he will have sufficient time to get set for any ruling.

Putout at first base. The mechanics here are far more complicated than one would think. The principles are to move as far as possible toward the pitcher's mound to a position about fifteen feet from first base *without obstructing the throw,* and to *get set* before making a decision. The base umpire moves farther toward the pitcher's mound when the throw is from the third baseman than would be the case on a throw from the second baseman or the shortstop. A position closer than twelve feet restricts the umpire's perspective. On these routine plays at first base, he should watch the ball as he moves into position and continue to watch the ball as it is thrown. *Just before the throw arrives* at first base, he should get set and quickly transfer his vision to the first baseman's base tagging foot to be certain that it is in contact with the base. The basis for his decision is then almost completely *audio*: which sound occurred first?—the ball striking the glove or the batter-runner's foot touching the base? Just at the moment of ball impact, the umpire should quickly glance from the tagging foot to the glove to assure that the throw has been held by the first baseman. In some cases, when the ball is "in the dirt," a slight hesitation is necessary before making the decision.

Attempts to steal second base. From a starting position behind and to the first base side of the pitcher, the umpire should watch the pitch, not the runner. As the umpire watches the catcher's throw, he should move parallel to the base line toward second base. *The first time that the umpire should see the runner is when the ball arrives at second base.* Inexperienced umpires have a tendency to take their eyes off the catcher's throw in order to glance at the runner—or even turn toward first base rather than toward second base as the play develops. There is no advantage whatsoever for him to observe the runner; on this play, as in most baseball plays, *nothing can happen without the ball.* As the tag is being attempted, he should get set on both feet and avoid signaling any decision on the run. If there is considerable impact at the moment of the tag and the runner appears to be out, the umpire should delay his signal momentarily in order to be certain that the fielder has not lost the ball.

Force double plays and sacrifice bunts. Considerable experience is required to enable the base umpire always to move in the correct direction

FIG. 3.2
Garvey Steals Second. Los Angeles Dodgers' Steve Garvey gets jump on New York Mets' pitcher Jim McAndrew and is successful in stealing second base despite tag effort of Mets' second baseman Teddy Martinez during third inning of game at Dodger Stadium in Los Angeles—29 April 1972 (AP Wirephoto).

on second-to-first double plays and on any sacrifice bunt play. The underlying principle is to move toward the base where the play will be the closest, which is usually first base.

Teamwork situations.   Umpires must constantly be ready to support and assist each other, in addition to carrying out their individual responsibilities. Following are the primary situations where the base umpires assist the plate umpire and vice versa:

1. *Did the batter swing?*   Since the plate umpire must concentrate his attention on the pitched ball, there are times when he is not able to rule accurately on whether or not the batter completed the swing. The batter must do two things to swing—cause the end of his bat to pass over home plate *and* clearly "break" his wrists. Frequently, the base umpire has a clearer view, and the plate umpire will step out in the direction of the base umpire to clearly indicate that he needs assistance on the call. The base umpire will immediately respond by signaling with a nodding of the head or by clenching his right fist to indicate a strike.

2. *Was the force or tag really made?* Either umpire can assist the other at any base on tag or force plays. A common example occurs when the plate umpire assists the base umpire on a tag play down the first base line, if the throw pulls the first baseman off the base. Frequently the plate umpire has a better angle to see whether or not such a tag was actually made.

3. *Fly ball putouts.* Obviously, in a two man game, one umpire must watch the catch and the other umpire the batter-runner tag first base. There must be agreement in advance as to who does what. Contrary to the advice of many umpire's associations, the advice here is that the base umpire always watch the catch and the plate umpire the tag.

4. *Plate umpire calls at third base.* Routine mechanics call for the plate umpire to make all decisions at third base when, with first base occupied, there is a base hit to the outfield. This arrangement provides for accurate initial coverage at first and second base (field umpire) and third base and home plate (plate umpire). If there is a decision made at third base by the plate umpire, the *base umpire* must be prepared to rule on any subsequent play at home plate! The plate umpire should move about half way down the third base line as the play develops and prepare to make any initial decision at either third base or home plate. The base umpire is ready to make any decisions at either first or second base and possibly to assist the plate umpire by making any secondary calls at third base or home plate.

FUNDAMENTAL SKILLS

Signals

Actually there are only four traditional signals used by baseball umpires:

1. A decisive right fist at eye level or higher indicates a *strike* or an *out*. (There is no signal for a "ball.")

2. Both hands extended from each side with palms down indicates that the runner is *safe.*

3. Pointing horizontally toward the center of the diamond indicates a *fair ball*; pointing toward either foul territory indicates a *foul ball.*

4. Both hands high overhead (or decisively waved past each other while overhead) indicates *time-out*, whether the time-out is necessitated by a request by a player or coach, a ground rule, interference or a *close* foul ball call, such as when a foul tip rebounds from the batter's front foot into fair territory.

Of more recent origin are two other hand signals:

1. The signal for a *home run* hit outside of the ball park—circling right forefinger just above the head level.
2. The signal for a barely deflected foul ball or foul tip—one hand quickly brushes the back of the other wrist and hand from wrist to fingertips.

Umpires coordinate voice signals with these hand signals. The principle is to use greater voice volume and greater hand signal decisiveness for close decisions than for obvious decisions. By withholding his emphatic voice and gestures for close decisions, the umpire "tunes himself" to the pace of the game and also reduces the chance of arguments on close decisions. It is suggested that the umpire *never* use his voice to call fair balls but only to call foul balls. This practice helps to prevent confusion.

Giving the Count
The plate umpire should routinely communicate the count on the batter (number of balls and number of strikes) whenever there may be doubt about the count. The lower the level of play, the more often the count should be given. The count is signaled by steadily holding up both hands, the fingers of the left hand indicating the number of balls and the right hand the number of strikes. Both fists closed indicate a "full" or three-and-two-count. One fist shows either no balls or no strikes. When three fingers are shown, the middle, ring and little finger should be used. Usually, the count is called as well as shown. The number of balls is called first, followed by the number of strikes. The best moment to give the count is immediately after the catcher has returned the ball to the pitcher; this is a good moment for attention. The voice should be loud enough to be heard and the signal steady and deliberate.

BASIC PENALTIES AND RULINGS

The intent here, as in other chapters, is to emphasize the essentials and to present a logical framework for better understanding of the rulebook itself. There is no substitute for concentrated study of baseball rules.

The Four Cornerstone Rulings of Baseball
There are four routine decisions in baseball: ruling whether each pitch is a *strike* or *ball*; whether each batted ball is *fair* or *foul*; whether each base runner is *safe* or *out* (only when a play is made on him) and, whether or not a batter is out because his batted fly ball has been *caught*.

At least ninety percent of all umpiring decisions involve one of these four decisions. The last of the four is usually a clear-cut, uncomplicated ruling: If any batted ball, fair or foul, is caught by a defensive player before the ball touches the ground or other fixed object, the batter is out.

The plate umpire shall call a pitch a "strike" if the batter swings and misses or if the batter does not swing and any part of the ball passes over any part of home plate between the batter's knees and shoulders. Thus, strikes may be categorized as "swinging" or "called" strikes. All other pitches which are not batted are called "balls" by the umpire. Contrary to the rules of baseball, shoulder-level pitches are habitually called balls, not strikes. The effective plate umpire strives for a consistent strike zone bounded on top by the batters uniform letters (about chest high) and at the bottom by the batter's knees.

Each batted ball is ruled to be a "fair" or a "foul" ball. A batted ball is foul when it is first touched, contacts any unnatural object, or leaves the park outside the foul lines, that is, to the right of the first baseline or to the left of the third base line. All other batted balls are ruled to be fair balls. All the bases, including home plate, are in fair territory. A ground ball bouncing directly over first or third base is a fair ball, even if the first bounce beyond the base is outside the baseline. When a batted ball is touched near the first or third base line, the *position of the ball,* not the position of the player, is the deciding factor.

The common reasons for ruling a base runner "out" are either when he is tagged by a defensive player while the runner is not in contact with a base, or when he is "forced" out. In force play situations, it is necessary merely for the defensive player to have the ball and be in contact with the given base. A force out situation is created when the batter batting a ground ball (or a fly ball which is not caught) and becoming a base runner "forces" runners to advance to the next base. Thus, plays made on the batter-runner attempting to reach first base are always force plays. No base runner except the batter-runner is forced if first base is not occupied. If all bases are occupied, a ground ball creates a force play at all three bases and home plate. If a *succeeding* runner is forced out, the "force" is removed for the *preceding* runners and preceding runners must be tagged.

PROBLEM CALLS

Baseball problem calls can be placed in two general categories: (1) calls where the complexity of the rule creates difficulty; and (2) calls where the complexity of mechanics creates difficulty.

Problem Rules

In addition to the four cornerstone rulings discussed in the previous section, five rule categories frequently create problems for the umpire. Rule book coverage of these five rules is difficult for the inexperienced umpire to comprehend, let alone to master to the point where the umpire can rule without undue hesitation in a game situation. The purpose of what follows is to introduce the difficult rulings to the prospective umpire. This must be supplemented by study of the rules, observation and discussion. The five selected rules categories are:

1. Interference and obstruction.
2. Appeal plays.
3. Balks.
4. "Book rules" for the awarding of bases.
5. Infield fly rule.

It is interesting to note that, while the four routine rule areas dominate the umpire's attention, very little of the baseball rules refer to them. The bulk of the written rules refer to the five rule categories listed above.

Interference and obstruction.   For the most part, baseball is a non-contact sport. Inevitably, however, physical contact between opposing players, a player and an umpire or a player and a spectator will occur. Frequently, as in basketball, these cases of physical contact, whether intended or unintended, will result in one team gaining an unfair advantage. On such occasions, a ruling is called for by the umpire in order to nullify this unfair advantage. For example, a catcher may contact the batter's swing, a base runner or base umpire may contact a batted ball before an infielder can make a play, the plate umpire may collide with the catcher who is attempting to make a play on the base runner, etc. Such situations can be complicated or simple, obvious or very negligible. While they occur rarely, especially where highly skilled players are involved, they *do* occur from time to time. The suggestions for the umpires are that they:

1. Know which is interference and which is not.
2. Anticipate interference situations.
3. Know the rule and the penalty.
4. Rule firmly without undue hesitation.

A delayed or weak interference decision almost inevitably will lead to an argument. For the purpose of definition, *obstruction* refers only to one situation: when a defensive player *who is not making a play* contacts a base runner; for example, a fielder who does not have the ball and is not playing the ball "impedes the progress" of the base runner. All other examples of illegal contact are commonly called *interference*. In all interference situations, regardless of who is involved, there are four basic questions to be answered by the umpire:

1. Who interfered with whom?
2. What is the penalty?
3. Is the ball dead?
4. Where are the other runners placed after the interference is ruled?

The following guidelines should be considered in making the call. The base runner has a "right of way" on the baseline in all cases *except* when a fielder is making a play on a *batted* ball, in which case, the fielder is "king" and all others must give ground. In almost all cases, there must be some form of *physical contact* before interference may be ruled; person to person, ball to person, equipment to ball, etc.

Appeal plays.   In certain play situations, the umpire(s) is required *not to rule unless the offended team appeals for a ruling.* Such situations are called appeal plays. Among the possible situations are the batter bats out of order, the base runner fails to touch a base or home plate and a base runner fails to "tag up" on a fly out. Appeal plays need not be a cause for particular concern if the umpire will pay heed to three principles which are always in effect during such situations:

1. The umpire must say or do nothing before the appeal to indicate to the offended team or anyone else that a successful appeal might be made.
2. No appeal may be granted *after the next pitch or after an intervening play* following the rule violation.
3. No appeal may be granted *if time is out* (for example: following a home run out of the park or a player's requested time out).

The ball must be in play at the time of the appeal.

Balks.   A "balk" is an illegal act by a pitcher when there is *at least one base runner on base.* Thirteen different types of balks are itemized in the rules, including such acts as faking a pitch and feinting a throw to first base without throwing to first base. The penalty for a balk is to advance *all* base runners (not the batter) one base. An illegal act by a pitcher with no runners on base is called an "illegal pitch." The penalty for an illegal pitch is to call a "ball" on the batter. The umpire cannot penalize a balk *without* base runners. He cannot penalize an illegal pitch *with base runners.* Many "balk moves" are borderline and difficult to detect. The best way to be able to distinguish between a balk and a near-balk is to have an expert demonstrate them. Merely reading the balk rules is not enough.

"Book rules." These refer to the number of bases awarded to base runners when a live ball goes out of play. The most important facet of the "book rule" is the overthrow. The award of bases is always *from where the play started* except when the overthrow was made from the outfield, in which case each base runner is awarded two bases from *where he was when the throw was released.* For example, if a base runner was just past second base and the batter-runner was not quite to first base when an overthrow from the outfield was released, a run would score and the batter-runner would be entitled to second base. In order to rule accurately on overthrows from the outfield, the umpire should "take a picture" of where the runners were when such throws were released. Whenever a live ball goes out of play, the umpires should immediately call "time" and award the bases as indicated. The "book rules" should not be confused with special ground rules which relate to the peculiarities of a given ball park.

Infield fly rule.   When all the requirements of an infield fly are met, any umpire should immediately shout, "Infield fly rule if fair, the batter is out." If this is called, the batter is out, and the runners are not forced to advance, whether the fly ball is caught or not. All of the following requirements must exist before this rule can be enforced:

1. First and second or first, second and third must be occupied.
2. There must be less than two outs.
3. A batted ball must be high in the air and, in the judgment of the umpire, it must be "easily handled" by an infielder.
4. It must be a ball that was batted, not bunted.

The only reason for this rule is to prevent the defensive team from converting this given situation into a force double play by intentionally failing to catch an infield fly. Fellow umpires should always remind themselves about the rule whenever first and second are occupied or the bases are loaded and there are less than two outs. A common reminder signal between umpires is for them to show each other *both thumbs* up in front of the chest area of the body.

Problem Mechanics

Rundown plays.   When a base runner is trapped between two bases by the defensive team, the rule of thumb is for the two umpires to take responsibility for the two "ends" of the play. The danger any time two umpires are involved in the same play is that one will rule "safe" and the other "out." The danger is usually eliminated if the decision is made only by that umpire who is at the end of the rundown where the tag is made. The other umpire *must not* make the decision unless asked.

Multiple base runners touching the bases. The golden rule of umpiring is to "watch the ball." Umpires also must strive to notice whether or not the base runners tag each base in the event that there is an appeal. On extra base hits with two or more base runners, it is difficult to watch both the ball and the base runners. Generally, the plate umpire observes home and third, the base umpire first and second. Basic vision remains on the ball until a runner nears a base, when the umpire glances quickly to determine whether or not the base was tagged and then once again watches the ball. When a base is missed, the umpire should mentally note which runner was involved, because he may not grant a possible appeal unless the runner, as well as the base, is identified by the appealing team.

Tag plays. The most difficult problem in a tag play is in attaining an adequate angle of vision so that neither the base runner nor the defensive player screens the umpire's vision of the tag. No matter how close he is to the play, he cannot see the tag if he is directly behind either player. The ideal angle would be between the runner and the fielder, more behind the runner than the fielder. The angle is even better if the umpire is *away* from the direction of the base runner's slide. Otherwise, his slide can screen the umpire's vision at the last moment. A brief delay on the decision is advised when the runner appears to have been tagged out; then the umpire doesn't have to change his decision if the ball subsequently is dislodged from the fielder. There is an explosive quality to a tag play, especially when it occurs at home plate. This tends to add to the importance of a correct decision.

Did the pitch hit the bat or the batter's hand? A common myth about baseball rules is that "the hand is part of the bat"—that the batter is not entitled to first base when a pitch strikes the batter's hand which is gripping the bat. This is a difficult play on which to rule. It is sometimes further complicated when the pitch seems to strike both the hand and the bat. The plate umpire must decide which the ball contacted first, the bat or the hand. Consider the following suggestions. If the sound is muffled, rule in favor of the batter; rule it a batted ball only if the sound *clearly* was that of wood, not flesh. When the umpire rules, he should signal his decisions as calmly and decisively as possible by:

1. Pointing to first base if the batter was hit by a pitch out of the strike zone; or
2. Brushing the back of his hand and signaling a strike if the pitch was in the strike zone or the batter swung at the pitch.

On extremely rare occasions, the pitch may rebound from the hand or bat to fair territory. If the pitch was in the strike zone or the bat was swung, such a rebound is a fair ball and in play.

OFFICIATING EVALUATED BY COACHES

What qualities do you appreciate in a baseball official?

ED BUSH—Los Angeles Valley College:

> Appearance, hustle, friendly but aloof, ability to listen to reason, clear and confident calls, consistent strike zone, proper positioning, knowledge of all phases of the game, dependable.

JOHN STEVENSON—El Segundo High School:

> He is consistent, firm and very pleasant to coaches and players alike. He is always in command of the game, but is definitely approachable for an explanation. He is so competent that I really hesitate to question his judgment.

JIM BRIDEWESER—Redondo Beach High School:

> He has left little doubt in anyone's mind as to his belief on the decision regardless of whether he was right or wrong. He lets you know he is convinced that his decision is correct.

HOWARD LOWDER—Chaffey College:

> Calm, strong calls—officials who do not decide the outcome of games.

ROSEY GILHOUSEN—Kansas City Royals:

> When the game was over, you asked yourself, "Who was the umpire?"

What qualities do you dislike in a baseball official?

JOHN SCOLINAS—Cal Poly, Pomona:

> 1. Chip on shoulder.
> 2. Cannot talk with him.
> 3. Making calls too soon.

ARCHIE ALLEN—Springfield College:

> Arriving late (just in time for the game), too authoritarian, inconsistency, talking to players or crowd.

RAY YOUNG—Stanford University:

> Inability to make decisions, too cocky or hardheaded.

Miscellaneous comments

RAOUL DEDEAUX—University of Southern California:

> All of us are looking for the official who loves this sport, has the ability to command respect and get along with people without having to flaunt his authority. He has to have a complete knowledge of the game and the hustle to be on top of every play and be completely oblivious to the sentiments and comments of the crowd. He is not intimidated by players and coaches.

JOHN HERBOLD—Lakewood High School:
> There are top umpires just as there are top players, coaches and others in the game—about five percent. But we must tolerate the other ninety-five percent. Good officials, like good hitters may be born and not made. Most umpires at our level have other jobs and cannot be expected to be fresh, rested and super officials. Good officials usually seem to be those who were knowledgeable players. Unfortunately, size does help, but it is not imperative.

DANNY LITWHILER—Michigan State University:
> Many umpires look for trouble and usually find it. These umpires are not sure of themselves and often miss plays because they have their head and mind on something else.

SKIP ROWLAND—Wilson High School:
> An official has to believe that *every game* they work is extremely important (as it is to the players, coaches etc.). They must come prepared to give a top effort and give a good honest job every time out. They must *enjoy* their work and be courteous and friendly in their dealings with all participants.

BILL ARCE—Claremont College:
> Basically we like to see officials remain somewhat removed from personnel involved in the contest. Backslapping, referring to players by name and holding conversations with players or coaches prior to, during or after the contest are not felt to be in the best interest of an atmosphere of unbiased officiating. We prefer a neat appearance, a professional attitude and a firmness which maintains command of the game without instilling the atmosphere of a drill sergeant. We prefer a man who has obvious knowledge of the rules and the intent of the rules, a love of the sport which is exemplified by his concern for the best interest of the sport, and who recognizes that interscholastic and intercollegiate sport must be conducted on educationally accepted terms. The task of the official is made more difficult when coaches do not accept their responsibility with regard to maintaining emotional control and physical control of participants. The good official must accept this additional responsibility when necessary to safeguard the future acceptance of athletic participation.

OFFICIATING EVALUATED BY OFFICIALS

What is the most difficult play to call in baseball?

BUD GRIFFITH—Southern California Baseball Officials Association:
> The steal of home and the half swing. Also since one cannot move as fast as the ball can be thrown, any play that might happen after the first play with bases loaded.

JOHN MORROW—Southern California Baseball Officials Association:
> The pulled foot of the first baseman when the official is on the infield or the slide by the base runner with the swipe at the runner when the umpire

is behind the play. The base umpire needs help from the plate umpire if the play is at first base.

LOU BERBERET—Southern California Baseball Officials Association:

Calling the overhand curve. Due to the break, sometimes pitches don't look like strikes.

What is the most difficult phase of mechanics in officiating baseball?

PAUL HUMISTON—Southern California Baseball Officials Association:

Attempting to give good coverage to the sacrifice fly that is hit to right field. The plate umpire must watch the catch from as beneficial a position as time and space will allow, but at best he will be required to make an educated guess as to when the runner tagged.

BUD GRIFFITH—Southern California Baseball Officials Association:

Such a large field of play and usually only two officials.

BOB WENTWORTH—Southern California Baseball Officials Association Former Professional Umpire, Six Years in Minor Leagues:

Pick off plays at first and third base when the base umpire is in the middle of the diamond with runners at first and third.

CARL ZIMMERMAN—Southern California Baseball Officials Association:

I don't believe the mechanics are particularly difficult for a hustling official as long as his partner also hustles. When one member of the officiating team "dogs" it, everything becomes more difficult.

Miscellaneous comments

DALE WILLIAMS—Southern California Baseball Officials Association:

I believe that it is very important to think ahead in baseball. In a two man system, you have to hustle and think ahead or you don't get the play covered. If one umpire is not thinking ahead, he sometimes gets the other umpire in trouble.

PAUL HUMISTON—Southern California Baseball Officials Association:

An instinctive approach to the game, acquired through much experience, is a plus factor of no little importance.

JOSEPH REED—Southern California Baseball Officials Association Instructional Chairman:

Trying to convince officials to hustle, work hard and take pride in their work is a problem that plagues us as instructional personnel.

GENE SMITH—Southern California Baseball Officials Association:

Most coaches and players you work for are great and realize that an umpire is a necessary part of the game. A few complain no matter who works the game. I am glad to say that they are in the minority.

MISCELLANEOUS CONSIDERATIONS

One Umpire Games

Many lower classified scholastic and community leagues cannot afford more than one umpire. In addition, there are times when one umpire is not able to work a game assigned to him, leaving the other man on his own. Most experts agree that the best place for one umpire is behind the plate, although some umpires prefer to move behind the pitcher when there are runners on base. The deciding argument is that the most crucial influence of an umpire is *calling balls and strikes*. Therefore, one umpire should sacrifice his accuracy on a few decisions on the bases to maintain consistency and control of the strike zone.

Opinions vary regarding the advisability of seeking a volunteer base umpire. Many umpires and coaches prefer one umpire rather than taking a chance on an untrained person. The suggestion here is to avoid the use of a volunteer umpire unless both coaches want a volunteer. If you work with a volunteer umpire, do not confuse him with excessive instructions. Try to get him in the right starting position before each pitch and give him support and encouragement between innings.

The Artistry in Plate Umpiring

There is much that outstanding plate umpires do to promote their own cause and the cause of a smooth-running and enjoyable game. Plate umpiring can either be a very lonely and thankless job or a cooperative and rewarding one, depending somewhat on the artfulness employed. Here are some suggestions:

1. Do not assert yourself any more than is necessary in order to keep the game going and under control.
2. Save your decisiveness in signals and voice for the close and crucial calls.
3. Take advantage of every possibility to promote good will and positive relationships without compromising your authority.

The plate umpire can also aid his cause by building sound relationships with those players closest to his work, the pitcher and the catcher—especially the catcher. He should communicate often with the catcher without interfering with the tempo of the game. He should encourage the catcher to "stay down" on low pitches. In a friendly but firm manner, he specifies to the catcher such routine matters as the number of warm-up pitches between innings and the method of getting the new ball into play. The pitcher's good will is almost as important as the catcher's, though more difficult to effect. Nevertheless, a feeling of near-comradeship frequently develops between a good plate umpire and a good pitcher; both are on their own, both have difficult jobs, both know that they depend somewhat on mutual goodwill.

Softball Rule Differences

Since softball field distances are shorter, the game seems faster. The emphasis in playing and umpiring softball is on anticipation and quickness. The basic rule differences are:

1. In softball, base runners may not leave their bases until the pitch is released by the pitcher; the runner is ruled out if he leaves the base too soon.
2. A foul fly caught by the catcher does not result in a putout unless the foul fly reaches an arc above the batter's head.
3. There are no balks in softball; regardless of whether or not there are any base runners, improper actions by the softball pitcher always result in "illegal pitches" (one ball on the batter and no advance by the base runners).
4. The pitch must be released in an underhanded motion. Although there are other interpretations of this rule, the most prominent is that "the wrist may be no farther from the side of the pitcher's body than the elbow."
5. When the pitcher starts his pitching motion, he must have both feet in contact with the pitcher's plate.
6. Before the pitcher starts his delivery, he *must pause* in some clear and consistent way and "present the ball" to the batter.
7. Before releasing the pitch, the pitcher's pitching hand may pass his hip not more than once.

When one considers that baseball and softball rules are very similar, it becomes clear that a baseball umpire has little difficulty adjusting to softball rules.

Softball Mechanics

In softball, the base umpire always takes a position behind the infield before each pitch, whereas in baseball the base umpire is to be found between the pitcher and the infielders whenever there are base runners. A position behind the infielders is necessary in softball to enable the base umpire to rule on the base runners leaving their bases early and to avoid interfering with normal movements of fielders and base runners within smaller areas. As in baseball, the softball base umpire immediately moves inside the infield area whenever the ball is batted or thrown into the outfield, so he can view both the ball and the runner(s) and so that the distance to be run by the base umpire is reduced.

Chapter IV

Basketball

THE GAME

Basketball is an active, fast-moving game complicated by a limited playing area. Difficulty in officiating the game involves being close to both the action and the players. This proximity invites spectator scrutiny on every play, something that does not exist in other team sports. For these reasons, basketball is an excitable game. With ten emotional players and two coaches, an emotionally stable official is a must.

Basketball is a game of judgments. It is felt that a minimum of from seventy to one hundred judgments will be rendered during one contest. Consequently, we probably witness only eight to ten calls per game that can be categorized as rule interpretation. Needless to say, the influence of the official is profound.

Officials may run one to three miles in working one game. Therefore, physical condition is very important. Constant, quick start-stop action requires stamina and endurance.

OFFICIALS AND THEIR RESPONSIBILITIES

The two floor officials are the referee and the umpire. They are assisted by a scorer and a timer located on the side of the court.

Referee

The referee is responsible for inspecting all equipment, which would include the court, baskets, the ball, backboards and the signaling devices of the scorer and timer. He should notify each captain three minutes before each half is to begin. The referee conducts the toss to start the game.

FIG. 4.1

Following the Ball. Brazilian players Adilson Nascimento (12) and Maciel Ubiratan Pereira (6) and U.S. player Dwight Jones, right, surround the basket during the preliminary round of the Olympic basketball tournament in Munich Wednesday. Douglas Collins of the United States watches the action in foreground. The Americans won, 61 to 54—31 August 1972 (AP Wirephoto via Cable from Munich).

As referee, he has the power to forfeit games and make decisions on situations not covered by the rules.

Officials

Neither official, referee nor umpire, has the authority to question decisions made by the other official. Other than the specific responsibilities outlined for the referee, the officials work the game as equals.

Scorer

The scorer records field goals made, free throws made and missed and a running summary of points scored by each team. Individual scoring is unofficial. The scorer records personal and technical fouls and time-outs. The scorebook of the home team is the official book. The scorer should use a horn or buzzer, unlike that used by the officials, to gain their attention.

Timer

The timer should have a stop watch or table clock as well as an electric scoreboard clock. The watch is used for timing intermissions, time-outs and backup for faulty scoreboard clocks. Timers may be called on to determine whether the ball was in flight before time expired. The timer should be cautioned not to sound the buzzer after the ball has been handed to a player to be inbounded.

MECHANICS

The officials must move constantly to secure the most advantageous position to observe the action. Stationary officials find themselves blocked out by the movement of the players. The official moving out ahead of the play while the players are moving toward the goal is referred to as the *lead* official. The official following the play and coming up the court in line with the offensive player in possession of the ball is called the *trail* official.

Division of the Court

We would like to suggest a division of the court whereby each official is responsible for one baseline and one sideline. When a foul is called, the officials should switch their end line responsibility, from lead to trail, allowing an opportunity for both officials to work under both baskets. The fact that all officials are not of equal ability makes it necessary to switch positions to offset the game from being unfairly influenced by one official working solely under one basket. Switching also alleviates the condition of overexposure of one official to the fans at one end of the

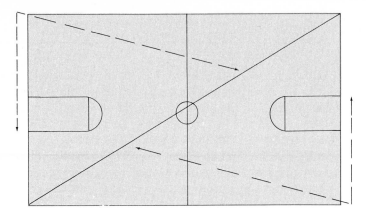

FIG. 4.2
Movement of the Lead and Trail Official

court. Several officials have suggested an overlapping principle where both officials attempt to watch all ten players. See figure 4.3.

Basic Movement

Movement direction is to the "base line right." When moving up and down the court as lead or trail official, the official must be cognizant of the positions of the players and the possibility of obstructing play. Therefore, it is essential that the official does not move to a lead position by a direct line to a position under the basket. Figure 4.4 illustrates the wide circling method of moving into position allowing the driving lanes to remain clear. The same applies to the trail official when the offensive team is moving the ball into the front court. He must stay slightly behind and

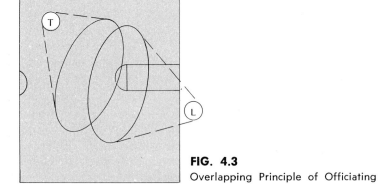

FIG. 4.3
Overlapping Principle of Officiating

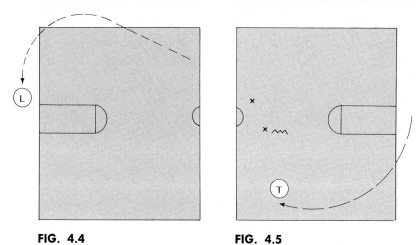

FIG. 4.4   **FIG. 4.5**

to the side of players bringing the ball up court to allow freedom of movement as shown in figure 4.5. By not getting ahead of the ball, the trail official is in a more advantageous position to retreat in the event of an interception. In summary, officials should make a conscious effort to stay clear of the action.

Jump Ball Situations

The two jump ball situations occur at the mid-court circle or the foul line circle. Movement of the officials is the same for both. The official opposite the toss, with his back to the scorer's table, should go with the ball and assume the lead position. This will allow the tosser to assume the trail position without obstructing play, as shown in figure 4.6.

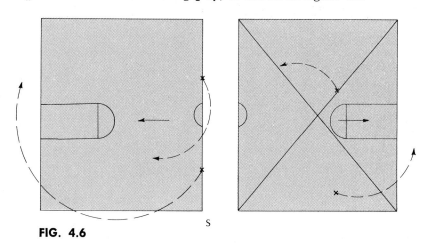

FIG. 4.6

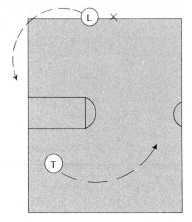

FIG. 4.7

Out-of-bounds Situations

When the ball goes out-of-bounds it is essential that the officials make is very clear which team will take possession. The nearest official should call "white ball" and point to the spot where he wants the ball to be put into play. If the player taking the ball out of bounds moves from the designated spot or it appears that there is some doubt as to whose ball it should be, the official handling the ball should call the ball back and order another inbounding. In figure 4.7, the lead official handles the ball on the sideline and moves to his position under the basket. The inbounding official must hold his position until the ball is inbounded or five seconds expires. In the pregame conference, the officials must agree on the procedure they will practice. In order to provide good coverage, they must actively assist each other by adjusting their position to meet the demands of the situation. New mechanics encourage "surrounding the inbounder" in out-of-bounds situations.

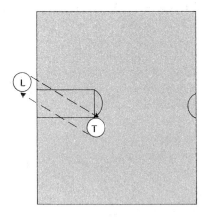

FIG. 4.8

Free Throw Situations

A commonly accepted practice, with minor modifications, works as follows: As each foul is called, the lead and trail officials switch positions. If the lead official is under the basket at the time the foul is called, he moves to the foul line to present the ball to the shooter and then assumes the trail position. The trail official moves under the basket, outside the foul line extended, and assumes the lead position. See figure 4.8.

Pressure Defense

The currently popular pressure defense calls for the close scrutiny of both officials. Pressure defense occurs when the defensive team closely guards the offensive team both as the ball is inbounded and all the way up court. When the back court and mid-court areas become congested, the officials must move to the best possible position to view the action. In figure 4.9, a compact coverage for observing the press is diagrammed. This is probably the only time officials should work almost opposite each other.

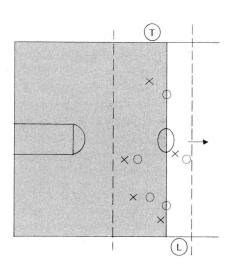

FIG. 4.9

FUNDAMENTAL SKILLS

Jump Ball

The official conducting the toss should split his feet with the front foot firmly planted. This will eliminate the tendency of the tosser to lean away from the circle. (The ball should be tossed above the jumping capability of the two jumpers.) The tosser must begin the toss at eye level, using one or two hands. This is a skill that must be practiced. He should not have the whistle in his mouth. This will eliminate the possibility of injury during the ensuing action by both teams to gain possession of the ball. The tosser must not move. He should remain stationary until the players are able to move around him without contact. The other official, facing the jump ball circle should determine whether the ball has been tossed properly, not too high or too low or to either side. If any of these situations occur, he should sound his whistle for a rejump. If this official does not make the call in an obvious situation, the tosser should sound his whistle as soon as possible.

Lead Official Watching the Flight of the Ball

Lead officials, at all levels of play, are guilty of watching the flight of the ball. While doing so, excessive rebound pushing and over-the-top contact goes unnoticed. The lead official must concentrate on observing baseline and rebound action. To accomplish this, his eyes must be down at all times. If the lead official is confident that the trail official is executing his responsibilities properly, he will not fall victim to watching the ball.

Procedure for Calling a Foul

Subject to variation, depending upon the area of the country or association the officials are affiliated with, the following procedure for calling a foul is recommended. Two methods will be discussed. First, when a personal foul is committed, the official should insist that the player charged with the infraction raise his hand; then the official should give the proper hand signal, report to the scoring table and then assume the lead position under the basket for the free throw. The other official will immediately get the ball and station himself at the free throw line in preparation for the free throw. He will then assume the trail position. The alternate method follows the same procedure with one exception. No matter which official called the foul, they will switch positions. See figure 4.8. Regardless of which method is adopted, the official underneath should stand outside the extension of the free throw line to avoid distracting the shooter. He should watch the players to his right or farthest from him to make sure that they do not come into the lane before the ball hits the rim on the shot. The outside official should watch the shooter and the players on the side away from him. If there are additional shots coming to the shooter, the underneath official or the lead official should return the ball to the outside or trail official, who will again present the ball to the shooter. He should also move down the center of the free throw lane and clearly indicate by hand signal and voice command how many shots will be taken and whether the ball is live or dead.

BASIC PENALTIES AND RULINGS

The categories of fouls and examples of each should be clear in the mind of every official. They involve personal and technical fouls.

Personal Fouls

Restrictions involve both offensive and defensive players. The major concern is that the player has freedom of movement. This would include holding, pushing, hipping, kicking and bending the body into other than normal positions. A player must make or cause contact to commit a personal foul.

Player control foul. This occurs when a member of the offensive team commits a foul while he or a teammate is in possession of the ball. With the exception of the double foul, this is the only circumstance when free throws are not attempted. The opposing team is awarded possession at the out-of-bounds spot closest to the infraction.

Intentional foul. This is a personal foul that could be classified as premeditated. Examples include the defensive man purposely holding or pushing the offensive man to slow or stop play or pushing the offensive man from behind when he has gained an advantage in a move to the basket. Two shots are awarded to the offended team.

Flagrant foul. This foul may be personal or technical and may or may not be intentional. If personal, violent physical contact with the intent to injure the opponent is evident, the offended player should be awarded two shots and the offender should be removed from the game. If technical, it involves vulgar and/or abusive conduct.

Technical Fouls

By team. A technical foul should be assessed to a team delaying the game, exceeding the allotted number of time-outs or having more than five men on the court.

By individuals. Unsportsmanlike conduct is the most common cause of the technical foul. Profanity, disrespectfully addressing an official and baiting an opponent are typical examples. Other violations might include attempting to gain advantage by interfering with the ball after a goal or by failing to pass the ball immediately to the nearest official when a violation is called.[1]

---

1. National Collegiate Athletic Association. *Basketball Guide* (Phoenix: Collegiate Athletic Publishing Service, 1973), p. 28.

PROBLEM CALLS

As indicated in the introductory chapter, our intent is not to examine all the rules. We will analyze some calls which are the most difficult to make according to contemporary officials.

Charging and Blocking

Charging and blocking should always be considered together. Avoidance of contact and established position are the major areas of concern. The dribbler must evade contact with a stationary defensive man by changing direction. Too often the dribbler is given the advantage when forcing his first step into the defender. The official must be aware of the possibility that the dribbler does not always have his head and shoulders in advance of the defender. If the defensive player has both feet down and takes a stationary position in front of and facing the dribbler, the dribbler is guilty of charging if contact is detected in the chest area between the shoulders.

FIG. 4.10
Charging

Blocking occurs when the defender moves into the path of the dribbler. Blocking may also occur when a player attempts to gain a better defensive position while moving toward the basket. If the dribbler and the defender are shoulder to shoulder, they must continue to move in a straight line. Any pressure contact exerted to crowd the dribbler to the outside will result in a blocking foul. The keys to the detection of blocking are first, defensive movement and secondly, the defensive man making contact with the side or shoulder area of the dribbler.

FIG. 4.11
Blocking

Unfortunately coaches teach defensive tactics to induce charging. Players taking illegal positions that do not allow the dribbler to avoid contact must be penalized.

Legal and Illegal Screen

A player setting a screen must assume and hold a position. When assuming this position, he must avoid contacting his opponent from the back and the side. He must allow his opponent to stop and change direction without creating contact. The speed of the player to be screened will determine where the screener may take position. The distance may vary from one to two normal steps from his opponent. Other complications arise when the screener moves into his opponent after taking his screening position. Since screening is a very important part of modern basketball, the officials must be prepared to differentiate between the legal and illegal screen.

Basket Interference

Taller players have increased the number of goal tending violations. The trail official, responsible for this call, must constantly work for the best possible position to view the trajectory of the shot. He should be concerned about the defender touching the ball above the level of the rim and on its downward flight. Too often goal tending is called prematurely as the ball does not reach the required height. Other considerations are the defender touching the ball, board or rim when the ball is on the rim or in the basket. A ball touched within the cylinder, which has the ring or rim as its lower base, is also construed as goal tending.

Traveling

Traveling has many facets. Because movement with the ball happens very fast, traveling ranks as one of the most difficult calls. The official must always be moving to improve his position to view and identify the pivot foot of the player in possession of the ball. A player receiving the ball while standing may pivot, using either foot as the pivot foot. After coming to a stop, he may lift either foot attempting to pass or shoot. The ball must leave his hand before he returns to the floor. Probably the best way to determine traveling is to get in step with the player. The observation of unnatural or uncoordinated movement of the feet usually indicates traveling. It is unrealistic to attempt to count the steps or establish the pivot foot in game circumstances. Shuffling the feet at the post and prior to the drive must be curtailed early in the game to offset carelessness. None of these can be detected if the official works too close to the ball.

Rebound Positioning

Rebound positioning is essential to winning in basketball. Both officials should be concentrating on this very crucial phase of the game because they are blocked out frequently. They should come to some agreement as to the degree of contact that will be allowed in screening out situations under the board. Players achieving proper rebound position must be protected. The inside man, or the man closest to the basket, has a definite advantage. The outside man, in order to get the ball, is forced to go over the top, which violates contact rules. The inside man, on the other hand, does not have the right to displace his opponent to improve

FIG. 4.12
Rebounding over the Top

his position. Both men, inside and outside, must go for the ball. Physically jumping into the opponent and then going for the ball is in violation of the rules. Unnatural positions of rebounders in the air or on the floor are usually the result of pushing. To promote continuity, it is not wise to call a foul on the outside man when the inside rebounder gains possession of the ball unless the contact is either too obvious or too severe.

Pressing Defense

In the era of the pressing defense, officials are confronted with the problem of keeping the defense "honest." Hand checking, "hipping," as well as moving into the opponent using the shoulder and chest, have become definite problems. The press requires better coverage of the backcourt. Consequently, the lead official should not assume his position under the basket when the ball has not passed mid-court. The lead official must come back and assist the trail official. Both officials are needed to cover the front or mid-court pressure defenses. With considerable movement on the part of both teams, contact is imminent. It must be remembered that the offensive team, as well as the defensive team, is entitled to freedom of movement. This includes the dribbler's option to pass off. The defender may attempt to block the pass with arms stretched upward and outward but may not make contact with the passer using any part of the body. At the same time, the officials must be conscious of blocking and illegal screens. When the press is broken, the lead official must be prepared to move quickly to his position under the basket.

Coming off the Ball Making Contact with the Shooter

During the course of the game, many fouls against the shooter are questioned by the spectators in what appears to be a blocked shot. They are right to a degree. The block is clean, but the ensuing contact with the body or hand coming off the ball creates the infraction. Unfortunately, many officials have a tendency to take their eyes off the shooter as soon as he releases the ball. It is imperative that the official watch each play to its completion to protect the shooter.

Establishing Control

There is a common misconception in regard to gaining control of a game in the opening minutes. Control can only be gained as a result of concentration—not overcalling or looking for infractions. Consistency is the key to control.

A physical game, on the verge of getting out of control, can be deterred. After lining up for a free throw opportunity, one of the officials should make a calm appeal to both teams to play basketball. This will usually suffice.

Lack of Sufficient Action

This rule is designed to offset stalling techniques practiced by out-matched teams. The key to the ruling is that the team behind is responsible for action while the defensive team is responsible if the score is tied. Officials should not be antagonized by the stall. It gives the underdog the element of surprise. Don't take it away from the coach if this is part of his game plan.

OFFICIATING EVALUATED BY COACHES

What qualities do you appreciate in a basketball official?

Fourteen qualities were mentioned by the coaches surveyed. They were background, humor, confidence, consistency, hustle, firmness, conditioning, receptiveness, reliability under pressure, courtesy, dependability, honesty, judgment and professional approach.

BILL SHARMAN—Los Angeles Lakers:
1. Top condition.
2. Good temperament.
3. Good judgment.
4. Thorough knowledge of the rules.

BOB BOYD—University of Southern California:
The official who is physically fit, confident, with good judgment and a background of athletics.

HOWARD LYON—Biola College:
The official who knows the rules, but uses discretion on calls. He keeps the game moving smoothly. He is punctual, pleasant and a hustler. He works well with the other official and he calls only what he sees.

LUTE OLSON—California State University, Long Beach:
The official who is unemotional and in complete control of his senses. He reacts in a gentlemanly manner which brings out the same in the coaches.

FRED SCHAUS—Purdue University:
Quiet but firm attitude towards players and coaches with complete control of the game.

What qualities do you dislike in a basketball official?

JOHN WOODEN—University of California, Los Angeles:
The "officious" type who looks for little technicalities and "hides behind" the rule book.

CHUCK KANE—Long Beach City College:
1. The official who draws attention to himself.
2. Overexaggerated calls.
3. Conversation following the game concerning how a team won or lost.

JERRY TARKANIAN—University of Nevada, Las Vegas:

The official who has a slow whistle, is influenced by crowd action and is not in position.

BILL FRASER—Long Beach City College:

Laziness, being too technical (unbending) and antagonistic (rabbit ears).

Miscellaneous comments

PETE NEWELL—1960 Olympic Basketball Coach, Los Angeles Lakers General Manager:

It is very important for an official to evidence an understanding of the players who are competing under great emotional and physical pressure and have patience with coaches and individuals who are peaked high emotionally because of the character of the game of basketball.

EDWARD S. STEITZ—Springfield College, Editor of the National Basketball Committee Publication of the United States and Canada:

The following statement presented by the Collegiate Basketball Officials Association best describes what the ideal official represents in the minds of both officials and coaches:

He notices everything, but is seldom noticed himself; he has the resourcefulness and initiative; he has dignity of voice and manners, but with no suggestion of pompousness; he is considerate and courteous without sacrificing firmness; he can control the players effectively and understandingly; he has a constant concern for the welfare of the players; he cooperates fully with fellow officials; he is physically able to be, and is, in the right place at the right time, and he knows what the rules say and what the rules mean.

HENRY P. IBA—Oklahoma State University:

The best basketball official who has worked for me knew exactly the rules printed but at the same time used good common sense on judgment plays. He respected the crowd, men competing in the game and the timer and the scorer. He made calls in such a manner that he was not the most important figure on the court; had the game under control from the beginning to the final whistle and never let the game get away from him by slowing up calls under the basket.

HOWARD DALLMAR—Stanford University:

The top officials that I have run into have the confidence of both teams. The players and coaches are only concerned about the game itself and not "what will the officiating be like!"

JOHN R. WOODEN—University of California, Los Angeles:

The coach has a grave responsibility toward the official and the official has a grave responsibility toward the coach, but, even more important, that each have a grave responsibility toward the game in every possible respect.

In the final analysis, perhaps the most important thing we need in all walks of life is more mutual trust, faith and understanding the problems of others.

If we could acquire and keep that, the coach-official relationship would cease to be a problem.[2]

OFFICIATING EVALUATED BY OFFICIALS

What is the most difficult play to call in basketball?

The officials surveyed were unanimous in their agreement that the most difficult calls are:

1. Charging and blocking.
2. Goal tending.
3. Illegal screens.

LLOYD LEITH—Former Supervisor of the Pacific 8 Conference:
Screen plays in and under the basket, goal tending, double foul situations, blocking and play away from the basket when a player is driving to the basket.

What is the most difficult phase of mechanics in officiating basketball?

Most officials surveyed felt that getting back to cover the fast break was the most difficult phase of mechanics.

DAVE MILLS—Southern California Basketball Association:
Lead official's view of the lane is often blocked as a maze of big men on offense clog up the middle.

WARREN SCOTT—Pacific 8 Conference Official:
Defenses collapsing underneath against poor shooting teams—defense lets them shoot and goes for the rebounds.

Miscellaneous comments

DAVE MILLS—Southern California Basketball Association:
There is no substitute for experience in becoming a capable official. Too many officials work after they have lost the physical ability to keep up with the game.

DOLPH SCHAYES—Ex-Commissioner of Officials, National Basketball Association:

The five necessary attributes of a good referee are:
1. Courage.
2. Ability to control the game.
3. Common sense.
4. Knowledge of the rules.
5. Rapport with players and coaches.

---

2. John R. Wooden, *Practical Modern Basketball* (New York: The Ronald Press Company, Copyright © 1966), p. 393.

Dᴀʀʀᴇʟʟ Gᴀʀʀᴇᴛꜱᴏɴ—National Basketball Association:

> The official with whom I like to work is one who is dedicated and thoroughly enjoys the game. He is the official who has the knowledge of the rules down perfectly, follows mechanics by the book and displays a genuine interest in *any* game.

MISCELLANEOUS CONSIDERATIONS

Officials' Conference

It is important for officials to arrive early for every assignment. This offers the possibility of meeting their working partner and coming to an agreement on basic mechanics, as well as allowing for an opportunity to discuss questionable rule interpretations. Getting to know each other before the game instills confidence. The ability to work as a team or unit will directly affect officiating performance. Discussion should include the pregame conference, half-time and post-game procedures. The mechanics and the method of switching, out-of-bounds coverage, pressing defense coverage and a determination as to whether each official is to call violations and fouls wherever and whenever he sees them should be clarified. The older and more experienced official should make it a point to talk to his working partner as an equal in order to establish his partner's self-assurance.

Postgame Procedure

Following the game, officials should refrain from conversation with either the winning or losing coach. The outcome of the game has been determined by numerous judgments. To defend any one call at this time would be neither feasible nor ethical. In the privacy of the dressing room, officials should take advantage of the opportunity to review specific game situations in an effort to become more proficient.

Controlling an Unruly Crowd

Situation control is a matter of experience. Having been confronted with similar circumstances in previous games, the official is in a position to make the judgment properly and without delay. Unsportsmanlike penalties are followed by ejections and finally default. The control of the crowd in unruly situations has not always been made clear. Initial signs of disorder and overt signs of rowdiness and game interference should be met with immediate action on the part of the school or recreation authority. Keep in mind that the game was designed for the participants. Troublemakers should be quickly escorted from the premises to avoid attention. Flagrant outbursts from larger groups should bring an appeal from the assigned authority using the public address system. A second appeal might be followed by clearing the gym for the remainder of the game or defaulting the game to the visiting team. Regardless of how the officials handle the situation, remember that basketball is an emotional game and patience and understanding must be exercised.

Scouting

Officials frequently scout their upcoming assignments to better prepare themselves. Conversely, coaches find that scouting officials is to their advantage by knowing the particular styles utilized by prospective officials. Becoming acquainted with officials' favorite calls, and for instance, seeing if they allow excessive contact in rebounding can afford the scouting coaches an opportunity to adjust their defenses and offenses. In addition, coaches should be cognizant of the areas of concentration discussed at officials' association meetings.

BIBLIOGRAPHY

National Collegiate Athletic Association. *Basketball Guide*. Phoenix: Collegiate Athletic Publishing Service, 1973.
Wooden, John R. *Practical Modern Basketball*. New York: The Ronald Press Company, Copyright © 1966.

Chapter V

Football

THE GAME

Football is a physical, combative sport pitting one player **against** another, or several, in some instances. Football can be an intense, emotional game. The increased size of the players, the advanced techniques and the general nature of the competition contribute to this intensity. Officials are expected to assist in the orderly progress of the game and to keep it free from flagrant and uncontrolled violence. Injury prevention must be foremost in the minds of football officials.

The greatest difficulty in officiating football involves gaining advantageous positioning. With twenty-two men in motion at the snap, officials are frequently screened out of the play. Consequently, they must be constantly moving and anticipating the movement of the ball and the action of the game to assume the best possible position in which to observe the play.

OFFICIALS AND THEIR RESPONSIBILITIES

Depending upon the level of competitive organization, the number of officials may vary from two to six men. The responsibilities for two, three, four, five and six man crews vary considerably. Coverage in this book is limited to the authorized federation or high school four man crew consisting of a referee, umpire, linesman and field judge.

Referee. The referee is the official in charge of the game. He has final authority in decisions not specifically delegated to another official.

Umpire. The umpire has primary jurisdiction over the legality of equipment.

FIG. 5.1
Troy Winslow (12) hands off to Mike Garrett on Southern California's second yard line in second quarter. Garrett moved it out the fourth line.

Linesman. The linesman has primary authority over legality of action in the neutral zone or on the line of scrimmage.

Field Judge. The field judge rules on action which is in advance of the other officials and is responsible for the timing of the game on the field.

General Procedure for All Officials

The official covering the runner is responsible for sounding the whistle when the ball becomes dead. Officials should use a marker to indicate that a foul has occurred. When an official detects an infraction, he should throw his marker, note the spot of the foul and the spot where the play ends. He should continue to concentrate on his responsibilities while the ball is alive. When the down ends, he should inform the referee of the foul, the status of the ball when the foul occurred and the offending team. The official detecting the foul should also give the preliminary signal. At the conclusion of the penalty procedure, the referee should face the offending team's goal and give the proper signals. The out-of-bounds spot is marked by the closest official who also signals time-out. The other officials should repeat the time-out signal.[1]

MECHANICS

A constant effort should be made to keep the play surrounded or "boxed in" at all times. Officials must exercise caution not to get too close or too far away from the play. The officiating crew must attempt to keep all players in vision without interfering with the players or the play. When the field judge was moved to the line of scrimmage to serve with the linesman as "referees" when the runner entered the side zones, it did improve in giving accurate "progress" marks on the ball and the runner. However, in some situations it was more desirable to have the field judge "off" the line of scrimmage. The flexible system of "on" and "off" mechanics is suggested. In a four man crew "on" mechanics are used unless a field judge informs the referee that he is moving to an "off" scrimmage line position or is directed to do so by the referee.[2]

Division of the Field
Sound mechanics will place the official in the right place at the right time to observe the action. Therefore, each official is positioned to best perform his responsibility. Scrimmage plays find the *referee* taking a position in the offensive backfield, several yards from the line of scrimmage. The *umpire* should take a position in the defensive backfield behind the middle linebackers. The *linesman* should assume a position in the neutral zone outside all players but as close to the ball as possible without interfering with the play. The *field judge* should be positioned near the neutral zone opposite the linesman. Basic positions for four official crews as suggested by the National Federation Athletic Association for the kick-off, running play from scrimmage, goal line plays and during try-for-point or field-goal attempt are diagrammed. See Figures 5.2 to 5.5.

Measurement for First Down
When a measurement is required, the referee should instruct the linesman to bring in the chains. The linesman should see that the chain is tightened toward the backward rod. The linesman should then grasp

1. National Alliance Football Committee, *1971 Official Football Rules* (Chicago: National Federation of State High School Athletic Associations, 1971), p. 77.
2. Jim Lineberger, "The Mechanics of Football Officiating" (Long Beach: Southern California Football Officials' Association, 1970), p. 3. (Mimeographed)

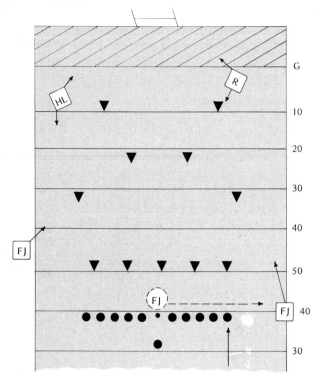

FIG. 5.2
Kick-off

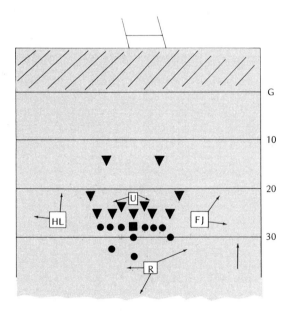

FIG. 5.3
Running Play
from Scrimmage

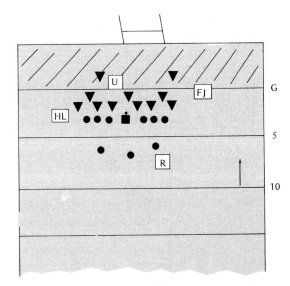

FIG. 5.4
Goal Line Plays

the chain at the chalk line nearest the backward rod at the rear of the line. The umpire should take the forward stake. When the linesman has placed the chain on the designated chalk line, the chain should be moved forward by the umpire. The referee determines whether or not the first down has been made. Any part of the ball touching or extending beyond the inside surface of the forward rod indicates sufficient gain. The referee should indicate by signal either a first down or the distance to be gained for a first down. When a first down is declared, the *linesman should always personally determine the point on the sideline at which the chain*

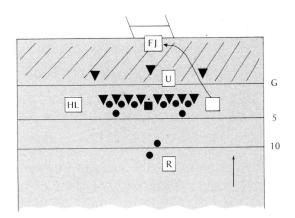

FIG. 5.5
During Try-for-Point or
Field-Goal Attempt

should be established. When moving the ball to the inbounds line because it is short of a first down, use the chains and the point on the chains to place it at the inbounds spot. The field judge should keep the players from both teams back and away from the measurement.

FUNDAMENTAL SKILLS

Calling Fouls (Penalty Flag)

When a foul is detected, note the number of the offending player, toss the penalty flag high into the air and mentally note the spot of the foul. *Continue to officiate but do not sound your whistle until the ball becomes dead.* When the ball is dead, the time-out signal should be given. Upon receiving the foul information from the official who called the foul, the referee should go to the approximate spot of enforcement facing the offending team's goal in preparation for the enforcement procedure.

Use of the Whistle

In football the whistle terminates the action. Therefore, the whistle must be kept out of the mouth. Inadvertent sounding of the whistle may result in the play being rerun. The whistle should be quick, loud and sharp, or sometimes consecutive short blasts when attention is not readily gained. Whistles should be sounded to protect the ball carrier who is clearly stopped. Sound the whistle *only* when you see the ball become dead. Otherwise you could be sounding the whistle on plays on the other side of the field. In the event of a fumble in this situation, the officiating crew may experience difficulty. Novice or new officials must guard against the temptation of the "back-up" whistle merely to become an active official.

Signals

It is suggested that the foul signal be given at the spot of the foul by the official calling it, and that the referee give it twice, once before enforcement and then after running off the penalty. The last signal should be given to both sides of the field from a spot in the clear and away from the ball. Give the signal once, then point to the offending team. *Don't make a show of it.* It should be emphasized that *all* officials repeat the time-out signal when given. Penalty and timing signals should be given in a deliberate and precise manner to assist the orderly progress of the game. For example, when the pass receiver catches a pass inbounds, give only the out-of-bounds signal. If a receiver catches a pass in the end zone and runs out of the end zone, signal only the touchdown. Confusion must be curtailed through deliberate, decisive signals.

Relaying the Ball

Officials should work as a unit to quickly retrieve the ball after each play. When retrieving the ball, a chain should be formed and the ball should be relayed to the new progress spot by short, underhand passes. The referee will then spot the ball and declare it ready for play.

BASIC PENALTIES AND RULINGS

There are one-hundred and seventy rule differences between the National Federation Athletic Association and National Collegiate Athletic Association rules. Consequently, penalties will be discussed in general terms.

5-Yard Penalties

These infractions include technical violations. Typical violations in this category are nonviolent infractions. They include offsides, illegal procedure, illegal motion, delay of game, intentional grounding of a forward pass and an illegal forward pass.

15-Yard Penalties

Personal fouls are the most prominent violations. Failure to enforce these penalties may result in placing the offended team at a disadvantage, losing control of the game and subjecting the contestants to possible injury. They include personal fouls, clipping, roughing the kicker, unsportsmanlike conduct, illegal use of hands by defense and offensive pass interference.

Live, Dead or Free Ball

When the referee signals the ball in play by sounding his whistle, it is considered a "live" ball. When the ball goes out-of-bounds, hits the ground on an incomplete forward pass or is otherwise called out of play by the referee, it is classified as a "dead" ball. A "free ball," sometimes called a "loose ball," exists when neither team has possession.

Enforcement of Penalties

The duties of the officials include detecting the violation of the rules, calling the violation and enforcing the violation. The offended team captain has the option of accepting the penalty or taking the down as played. The suggested procedure is as follows:

1. As soon as the ball becomes dead, give the time-out signal and make certain that one official is holding the dead-ball spot and that the down box and chains are not moved.

2. If the offended team captain's most advantageous choice is obvious, enforce the penalty *without consulting him. Run off the penalty.* (It looks awkward to see a referee approach a defensive captain saying, "If you refuse the penalty it will be a first down for the offense at this point." It would be much better to explain it to him afterwards if he does not understand than to delay the game when the most advantageous choice is obvious.

3. Give a clear signal for the foul committed; face the offending team's goal: calculate and *visualize* the distance to be penalized (avoid stepping off the penalty) and then run off the penalty; repeat signal for foul committed; spot ball; get ready-for-play signal from captains; and declare the ball ready-for-play.

4. Notify the offending team's captain of the foul called and the number of the offending player. On any 15 yard penalty give this information to the linesman and the field judge so this may be relayed to the offending team coaches.

5. If the choice is not obvious, go to the approximate spot of enforcement, call both captains together; face offending team's goal; give a clear signal of foul or fouls committed, pointing with both arms toward offending team's goal; notify captain of the foul committed; explain options to the offended team captain.

6. If the penalty is accepted, go to the spot of enforcement, run off the distance to be penalized; call for the ball from the umpire and spot the ball.

7. After penalty is completed take a position in the clear where you can be seen. Give signal to each side of the field.

8. If the penalty is declined or if the fouls are offsetting, call for the ball and see that it is properly spotted. Then take a position in the clear where you can be seen. Give the "penalty declined" or "no play" signals to each side of the field.

9. Get each captain's ready signal and declare the ball ready-for-play.

10. In case multiple fouls are called, inflict distance penalty for the first foul; place ball on the ground; give proper foul signal; pick up ball; inflict distance penalty for second foul; give proper foul signal; spot ball; get ready signals from captain; declare ball ready-for-play.

11. If the defensive team fouls on a successful try-for-point *that is not to be repeated, but to be enforced on the succeeding kickoff,*

give the extra point signal, then turn and face the center of the field and give the foul signal that is to be enforced from the 40 yard line. The field judge gives the foul signal before running off the distance penalty and then repeats the signal from the new spot.

All officials in the crew should check the correctness of the penalty. When conflicting opinions exist, justice requires that the ruling be withheld until an attempt is made to establish a common ground. If it is a case of the down box being moved or having a questioned down appearing, utilize the press box statistics man to determine absolutely the correct situation. *Remember not to rush into a wrong decision; it is much better to take a little time and come up with the correct answer.*[3]

PROBLEM CALLS

A basic understanding of the principles of enforcement and general rules should limit the number of problem calls.

Pass Interference

It must be remembered that both offensive and defensive players may make a play on the ball at the spot of completion or interception. Both the offensive and defensive players must make a legitimate attempt to play the ball—not the man. If no advantage was gained, interference should not be called. Therefore, violent contact may occur without penalty. The two key questions are:

1. Did one player interfere with the other player's opportunity to make a play on the ball?
2. Did he play the ball or the man?

A defender can bump or slow down a potential pass receiver before the pass is released if he does it without roughness and not more than once on any given play. However, *pass receivers may not be bumped or pushed when the ball is in the air.* If the players are side by side, don't call pass interference for tripping unless one player trips deliberately or while playing the man rather than the ball. *Offensive pass interference may occur any time after the snap* and until the pass reaches a receiver or defender. The rule on offensive pass interference is especially difficult to enforce when the initial play action appears to be a running play but suddenly becomes a pass play.

3. *Ibid.,* p. 15.

Tackle Eligible Play

This play is very difficult and must be clearly understood. Know your numbers and carefully observe the actions of the offensive backfield. In college football, offensive players numbered 50-79 are normally classified as ineligible pass receivers. These players may not advance beyond the neutral zone until the pass is thrown. In high school football, the tackle is eligible if he lines up at the end of the line of scrimmage with no more than four teammates behind the line of scrimmage. After a defensive player touches a forward pass, all players become eligible receivers.

Fouls During the Kicking Game

Fouls occurring on kicking plays when the ball is free requires careful scrutiny by all members of the officiating unit. Advantageous positioning and movement are essential for total field coverage in this "loose" ball situation where the potential for infractions is the greatest. Twenty-two players in motion provide numerous possibilities for infractions and/or injury. The incidence of clipping and crack-back blocks is most obvious in kickoff and punt returns.

Late Hitting

Avoidance of injury is an important responsibility of all officials. Hitting an opponent after the whistle, roughing the kicker or passer and spearing must not be tolerated. Prevent injuries by getting to the ball immediately after it has become dead. Players must be constantly reminded about playing the whistle, or ceasing action, to alleviate unnecessary injury. Being continually alert throughout the play and continuing alertness after the play terminates will aid this effort. Officials should be encouraged not to merely mark the out-of-bounds spot but to talk the players out of fouling out-of-bounds as well.

Offensive Holding

Too often plays leave the neutral zone with the offense guilty of holding. The umpire must concentrate on the actions and reactions of both lines before dropping back to cover the middle passing zone. The hands must be in contact with the blocker's body and kept below the shoulders of the opponent throughout the block. The blocker's forearms must not move out ahead of his shoulders. Such action may result in offensive holding. Holding is defined as using a hand or forearm, unless the hand is kept in contact with the blocker's body and below the opponent's shoulder.

Holding also occurs when an offensive player uses his arms to hook, lock, clamp, encircle or lift an opponent.[4]

Roughing the Passer

Many quarterbacks have the ability to quickly release the ball just before a defender makes contact. Consequently, it is difficult for the on-rushing defender to avoid hitting the quarterback after the pass has been thrown. The official must determine whether the defensive player could have sufficiently controlled his momentum to avoid contact. There is a natural tendency for the inexperienced football official to be too ball conscious. Since most fouls occur away from the ball, officials who watch a pass in flight are not providing coverage.

Clipping

Much like late hitting, this call must be made to minimize injury. A player may not run or dive or hit an opponent by throwing his body from the rear or to the back of the legs. Injury incidence is highest when a player cannot prepare himself for "blind side" contact. The official must observe the initial contact to determine whether the opponent could have seen or evaded the blocker. The "legal clipping zone" is four yards laterally and three yards longitudinally in each direction from the middle lineman, or in other words, eight yards by six yards. After the initial charge, the runner must be protected against the clip. In order to call clipping correctly and consistently, the initial contact must be observed.

Neutral Zone Infractions

The space between the scrimmage lines of the offense and defense is approximately eleven inches or the length of the football.[5] Offsides must be called on the player who initiated the movement in the neutral zone. Movement of an offensive or defensive player that causes contact due to the reflex action of his opponent is an offsides infraction. Any encroachment in the neutral zone to hinder or deceive an opponent must be penalized.

Grabbing the Face Mask

Coaches and players have become very conscious of this foul in recent years. As a result, claims are often made when the foul did not, in fact, occur. Only tackling the face mask is illegal; tackling the chin or the

---

4. National Collegiate Athletic Association, *Football Guide* (Phoenix: College Athletics Publishing Service, 1972), R28.
5. *Ibid.*, p. R9.

headgear is not a foul. The official must realize that face mask fouls can cause serious neck injuries; therefore, this infraction must be rigidly and unhesitatingly enforced.

OFFICIATING EVALUATED BY COACHES

What qualities do you appreciate in a football official?

John McKay—University of Southern California:

1. Integrity.
2. Competed in the sport.
3. In good condition.
4. Thorough knowledge of the rules.
5. Poise.

Bob Devaney—University of Nebraska:

Honesty, courage and good eyesight.

John Ralston—Denver Broncos:

Number one is courage of convictions. Right or wrong, the official that makes a clear-cut decision is the man that I like to have working our games. Also, I like to see the game moving along, and in the best interests of the players participating. It is important that the official explain thoroughly any decision that is questionable to the team leaders on the field. He should always keep in mind that keeping the game moving is the most important thing, with as little flair for the spectacular as possible.

Paul Chafe—Long Beach City College:

Control, education rather than call, consistency, knows differences between high school and college rules, rule changes and polite interpretations.

Daryll Royal—University of Texas:

The official that takes charge, keeps the game under control and never loses his poise.

Len Casanova—University of Oregon:

The official who can explain, in *simple* language, options in a penalty situation to the offended team captain.

Tom Prothro—Los Angeles Rams:

Friendly, efficient, hardly aware that he was there and willing to freely admit occasionally that he was wrong.

What qualities do you dislike in a football official?

John Pont—Indiana University:

Indecision and trying to correct a bad call by trying to make up for it a little later.

STAN PAVKO—Modesto City College:

Being a dictator, being a homer, apple polishing with coaches and administration, rabbit ears, trying to show up his fellow officials, guessing on calls, hot temper and officiating only for monetary gains.

VIC ROWAN—San Francisco State College:

Making calls when seeing only part of the foul.

GARY JACOBSEN—Long Beach City College:

Surley, non-communicator, antagonistic, red neck.

LEE EISEN—City College of San Francisco:

Over-officiates, unapproachable, lazy, too much of a take-over man trying to officiate all positions.

Miscellaneous comments

HAL SHERBECK—Fullerton Junior College:

Too many officials work just for the money that can be made. They have no feeling for the game and the boys who are playing. There is no room for the official who thinks the audience came to watch him. This official takes the game away from the ball players, usually is short tempered and with little understanding. Personal feelings against a school cannot enter into officiating.

JOHN McKAY—University of Southern California:

Most poor officiating today is the result of the huge demand of hundreds of schools. More attention should be given to the proper training of officials by clinics or associations designed to bulk up the number of qualified officials.

ERNIE JOHNSON—Cerritos College:

The most disturbing thing in line officials is the ever increasing tendency for them to attempt to even up these one-sided games. An official's job is to control the game and interpret the rules. A team should not be penalized because they are superior.

VIC ROWAN—San Francisco State:

The trouble in officiating today is getting young men a chance to work enough to get the needed experience to move up the ladder.

JIM CHEFFERS—Los Angeles City Schools:

Officiating is a state of mind. Your top officials have a terrific attitude toward the game and officiating. These men put in hours of studying rules and mechanics as well as physical conditioning.

ROD ENOS—Whitworth College:

I never complain on what the officials call. I do complain about what the officials do not call, especially when it is obvious or a game becomes one sided and the officials are in a hurry to end the game.

OFFICIATING EVALUATED BY OFFICIALS

What is the most difficult play to call in football?

Football officials surveyed are most concerned about the following calls:

1. Pass interference.
2. Deliberate grounding of the pass.
3. Clipping—crackback blocking.
4. Quarterback being hit from the side and deciding whether the arm went forward for incomplete pass or if it was a fumble.

What is the most difficult phase of mechanics in officiating football?

Most often mentioned by the officials in the survey were:

1. Being in the right place at the right time.
2. Covering side and flank zones and the deep pass play.

Miscellaneous comments

JACK NEWMAN—Southern California Instructor:

It has been my experience (20 years) that a very large majority of officials *do not know the rules.* How do they continue to work? They work because they take positions other than the referee and "lean on him" during the game. They continue to work because of the desperate need for officials in Southern California High School games. The demand outweighs the supply! As we "go up the ladder" (Junior College and College) this problem becomes less and less crucial but still exists to some degree.

JIM LINEBERGER—Southern California Football Officials Association Instructional Chairman, Pacific 8 Umpire:

You can teach a new official football rules, and where to be, and what to look for on various play situations (mechanics), but it is very difficult to teach him good judgment and to teach him an overall "feeling for the game." There is no place on the field for the official that enforces the rules only by the "letter of the law" unguided by good common sense. It is essential that the beginning official quickly learns preventative officiating techniques and applies common sense values to all of his judgments and decisions. My definition of an "experienced official" is one that has made mistakes personally in the past, or observed them in others, and he has the capacity to *never make that same mistake again in the future.* It is my observation that there will always be a need for good experienced football officials at all levels of competition.

JIM TUNNEY—National Football League:

To be selected to officiate in professional sports is the goal of every official. Those fortunate enough to have been selected have realized a goal of hard work, sacrifice and dedication. The financial remuneration given to an official should always be a secondary factor in one's interest in becoming an official. The primary factor should be a sense of belonging and feeling of participation in the sport. If it is not held first and foremost, one will never be truly successful in officiating.

BUD BRUBAKER—National Football League:

> Coaches should be cautious not to criticize officials in front of players and spectators. I would rather work with an official with good mechanics than good knowledge of the rules. The referee can assist on the rules, but not mechanics.

ROSEY GILHOUSEN—Southern California:

> Throughout 38 years, I have found no substitute for experience; however, if I were a young man starting again, I would observe every crew for hints on how to improve my mechanics. You can learn rules from books. Mechanics come through observation and experience. If you are out of position, you are the weak link in the chain of a good team.

NORM DUNCAN—National Football League:

> To be a successful football official, one must have a spirit for the work. To have played the game and have a desire to get back on the field is not enough. Regardless of the level, high school, college or the professional, the truly outstanding official must have a driving force to excel in rule knowledge, mechanics and attitude toward players. To excel in the rules is to be creative in your study and imagination. You must be able to look beyond the printed page and develop a *true feeling* for the *intention* of each and every rule. *Your thinking* will *guide* your *actions* on the field.

NORM SCHACHTER—National Football League:

> Experienced officials are most essential. The realization that all positions in a crew are as important as any other should be kept in the mind of all. Crew conference prior to the game "is a must" especially if it is different men each week.

MISCELLANEOUS CONSIDERATIONS

Referee's Pregame Conference Check List

1. Discuss any unusual plays or formations received from the coaches, and *all record* the names, numbers and positions of the captains.
2. Review pertinent rules and interpretations. Invite questions from fellow officials.
3. Review and discuss the following mechanics:
   a) Retrieving and handling the ball on incomplete passes and out-of-bounds plays, marking punts going out on the fly.
   b) Methods of spotting the ball.
   c) Handling fumbles.
   d) Coordinating use of whistle at end of quarter between official charged with timing and the referee.
   e) Position and coverage on:
      (1) Kick-off.
      (2) Time-outs.

(3) Running plays.
(4) Forward passes.
(5) Punts and run backs.
(6) Man-in-motion.
(7) Goal line plays.
(8) Sideline plays.
(9) Out-of-bound plays.

4. Each official should present questions on rules and mechanics.
5. Discuss procedures for calling fouls and exacting penalties.
6. Review the following signals:
   a) Touchdown.
   b) Dead ball.
   c) First downs.
   d) Fouls.
   e) Progress.
   f) Time-outs, especially on punts out-of-bounds.

7. Reporting method of substitutes *if not free substitution.*
8. Method of rechecking each other on decisions.
9. Communications between officials and words to be used like:

   a) "Close, close."
   b) "Dead ball, dead ball."
   c) Foul during "loose" or "free" ball.
   d) Foul during "scrimmage kick" or "incompleted pass."
   e) One-half distance penalty—"inside the 10"; "inside the 30."

Communication

In order to promote cooperation with both coaches, it is imperative that the linesman and the field judge working closest to the sidelines have a complete understanding of each infraction. This will enable either of these officials to respond to the coaches' questions regarding the infraction. The coach is entitled to information regarding the nature of the foul and the player who committed the infraction in order to correct individual player mistakes. Denied this communication, the coach is hampered in his attempt to make the necessary adjustments. If the sideline official cannot explain the infraction, he should immediately approach the referee and relay the information that is in question.

General Procedure for Becoming a Football Official

Interested individuals must first join their local officiating association. The Association will make available, as a part of the membership dues, a kit of instructional materials which will include a study guide, rule books, mechanics book and a case book. Association training programs feature required meetings, field work clinics, actual scrimmages, classification and other written examinations. Successful candidates are then classified. A qualified list is forwarded to the area commissioner whose office is responsible for making the actual game assignments.

Official Ratings

Officials are continually rated by coaches, senior fellow officials and Association instructors to determine their strengths and weaknesses. This

TABLE 5.1

Football Official's Rating*

	Official's Name			Date	
	Game	vs		Classification	
	Visitor		*Home*	A, B, C, etc.	
	GOOD 10	FAIR 5	POOR 0		
General appearance					
Uniform					
Punctuality					
Personality					
Attitude toward football and/or officiating					
Mechanics					
Rules knowledge					
Signals					
Use of the whistle					
How does he accept constructive criticism?					
Sub totals					
					Total

In your opinion is he ready to work:

Varsity	90-100	Outstanding prospect
	80-85	Good prospect
Bee	60-75	Average prospect
	30-35	Needs improvement
J. V.	0-25	Poor prospect
None Yet		

Which position?   REF   UMP   H. L.   F. J.

Additional Information on the Other Side:

Referee's Signature

* Jim Lineberger, "1972 Instructor's Notebook Outline Guide," (Long Beach: Southern California Football Officials' Association, 1972), Appendix. (Mimeographed)

procedure assists the commissioner's office in making future assignments. Capable, qualified and experienced officials are rewarded for their dedicated efforts by being assigned to important games and higher level competition.

BIBLIOGRAPHY

Lineberger, Jim. "Mechanics of Football Officiating." Long Beach: Southern California Football Official's Association, 1970. (Mimeographed)

———. "1972 Instructor's Notebook Outline Guide." Long Beach: Southern California Football Official's Association, 1972. (Mimeographed)

National Alliance Football Committee. *1971 Football Rules Book.* Chicago: National Federation of State High School Athletic Associations, 1971.

National Collegiate Athletic Association. *Football Guide.* Phoenix: Collegiate Athletic Publishing Service, 1972.

National Football Committee. *Football Official's Manual.* Chicago: National Federation of State High School Athletic Associations, 1971.

Chapter VI

Swimming

THE GAME

Swimming is the only sport in which technique may determine the outcome of the competition. To be more specific, improper stroke technique should disqualify the contestant. Much the same as in track and wrestling, the referee-starter may have inclusive responsibility to include the start, stroke and finish.

OFFICIALS AND THEIR RESPONSIBILITIES

Referee
The referee has complete jurisdiction over the meet. He must enforce the rules and assume the responsibility for making all official assignments. The referee has the authority to expedite the meet with a minimum number of delays.

Starter
The starter has control over the contestants after they have been assigned to him by the referee. In most dual meets, one man may serve as referee-starter and perform the duties of both officials. The starter is responsible for preparing the contestants for each race by explaining the stroke requirements and the number of laps to be swum.

Lane Judges and Timers
When completely automatic judging and timing equipment is available and is functioning properly its results will be considered as primary and official information. In case of malfunction, secondary information

FIG. 6.1

Churning His Way to Olympic Record. Tom McBreen of San Mateo, California, works his leg of the 400-meter freestyle relay in Munich Thursday. The U.S. Team broke the Olympic record for the event with a time of 7:46.42—31 August 1972 (AP Wirephoto via Cable from Munich).

from a semiautomatic timing and judging device with one or more officials per lane or the prescribed ballot system or modified ballot system should be used. If the ballot system or automatic timing and/or judging device is not used, judges are designated to pick the first three places and three timers are assigned to first place in dual meets. In championship meet trials, three timers are assigned to each lane. In championship finals, two lane judges and three timers should be assigned to each lane.[1]

Take-Off Judges

For the purpose of judging whether the second, third and fourth swimmers are still in contact with the starting mark when his teammate touches the end of the pool, a take-off judge is assigned to each relay team.

1. National Collegiate Athletic Association. *Swimming Guide* (Phoenix: College Athletic Publishing Service, 1973), p. SW-29.

Clerk of Course

The referee-starter's most important aide may be the clerk of course. In dual meets, this responsibility is commonly assumed by the athletic director or the coach of the host school who serves as referee. The clerk should check each swimmer into his assigned lane. His effectiveness will determine how well your meet will run.

Stroke Inspectors and Turn Judges

Assigned officials report violations of stroke and turn to the referee-starter who will in turn disqualify the swimmer. In most dual meets, this responsibility is assumed by the referee-starter.

Diving Judges

For dual meets, diving competition requires a minimum of three judges, an announcer and a secretary. Championship meets require a minimum of five judges, an announcer and a secretary.

Scorer

General practice finds the administrative effort a function of the host school or club, regardless of the level of competition. The scorer should delegate recording-announcing and scoring responsibilities and supervise their efforts. The referee should insist on an intelligent scorer for prompt, accurate and immediate posting of running scores.

Runners

To coordinate the finish and immediate scoring of each event, runners carry the results, which are recorded by the judges and timers, to the scoring table.

MECHANICS

In the restricted area of the pool deck, mechanics become especially important. All officials must confine themselves to their respective work areas. The starter must keep the sides of the pool deck clear for observing strokes, turns, take-offs and finishes. Elevated stands should be situated on both sides of the finish to provide an unobstructed view for the judges. Dual meet timers should assume a position on either side of the finish to determine first place. Championship meet timers should be placed directly over their assigned lane at the finish. Finishes of swimming races in the shorter distances are decided by inches. Therefore, it is necessary to continually work for the best possible position in order to view the

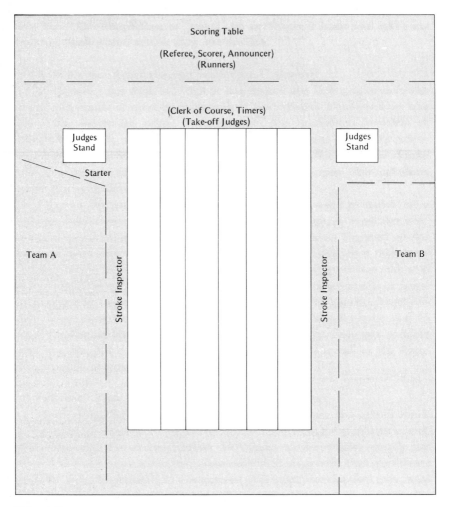

FIG. 6.2

finish. It is advisable in many pools to have the area around the starting blocks and near the scoring table roped off and restricted to officials only. Bright colored caps are recommended as a means for identifying the officials.

FUNDAMENTAL SKILLS

Starting Procedure

The starter must strive for an equitable start for all competitors. With the exception of the backstroke, all races start from a standing position on the starting blocks. When the command "take your marks" is given,

FIG. 6.3
Swimmers!

FIG. 6.4
Take your Marks!

all swimmers should assume their starting position. When the starter sees that all swimmers are motionless, he starts the race with the *pistol shot.*

Timing

Each watch should be tested prior to the race to determine its reliability. This can be accomplished by starting the watches simultaneously by pressing the stems together. A timer should familiarize himself with his watch by starting, taking the slack out at the stem, stopping and resetting the watch. To avoid damage to the watches, the referee should prewind all watches and inform his timers that he has done so. Cords for wearing the watches around the neck should also be provided. Timers should be alerted to clear their watches before each race. This should be executed at the command of the head timer when he receives the ready signal from the starter. Each timer must take the slack out of the watch, at the stem, at the start and the finish to record an accurate time. The index finger is faster than the thumb and its use is recommended. How the watch is started and stopped may determine whether the swimmer will place. Following the race, watches should not be cleared until the head timer has had an opportunity to read them and record an official time. Utilizing three watches the official time is determined. See figure 6.5.

Judging

In dual meets, a minimum of two judges will pick first place and one each for second and third places. Pending disagreement among the judges, the chief finish judge must follow numerical order. For example:

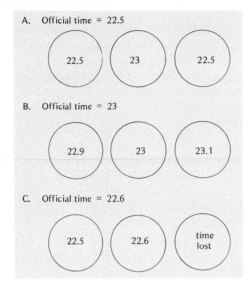

A. Official time = 22.5

22.5   23   22.5

B. Official time = 23

22.9   23   23.1

C. Official time = 22.6

22.5   22.6   time lost

FIG. 6.5
Determining Official Time with Three Watches

if first and second place judges both select contestant A, the decision of the first place judge is final.[2] In championship meets, two judges are assigned to each lane. Positioned on opposite sides of the finish, each judge independently determines where the contestant in his lane finished and records it on a card as shown in Figure 6.6. Timer's and judge's cards shall be the same color for each respective lane. Using the ballot system, the finish is determined by adding the numerical value of the three ballots of each lane (two ballots for finish and one ballot for time). The swimmer with the lowest numerical total is declared the winner.[2]

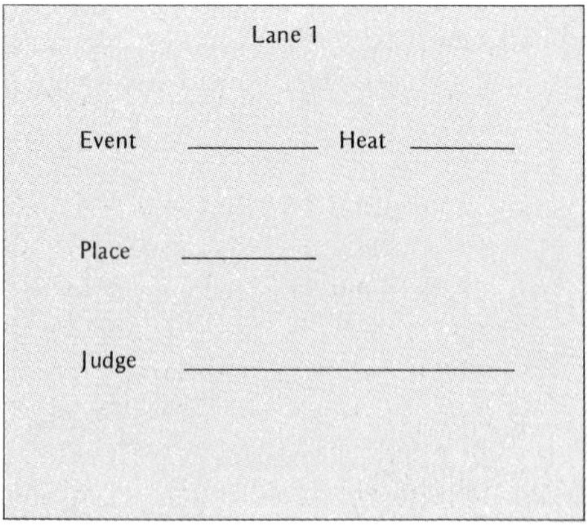

Lane 1

Event _____ Heat _____

Place _____

Judge _____

FIG. 6.6
Ballot Card

2. *Ibid.*, p. SW-32.

Take-off Judging

The method for judging relay take-offs is performed manually by the judge placing his little finger in contact with the longest toe of the next swimmer. The take-off judge should concentrate on observing the touch of the incoming swimmer before finger contact is broken by the swimmer leaving the block. When automatic equipment is used, back-up judging is based on visual judgment.

Judging the Diving

Preferably, one or more of the diving judges should have had diving experience. If this is not the case, the judges of the dive must take it upon themselves to study the scoring procedures intently. Each dive is categorized by its predetermined degree of difficulty and the score is computed by multiplying the total scores of the judges. Points are awarded from zero to ten. The judges must consider the forward approach, the take-off, the execution of the dive in the air and the entry into the water. Attention must also be directed to the position announced for the dive. The dive may be done in layout, pike or tuck position. Judges must be alert to discern whether the diver has taken a minimum of three steps and has executed the dive in the air, not the board. After each dive, the whistle is sounded by the referee. The judges simultaneously flash their awards from a scorebook. The announcer reads the individual awards. After all the scores have been read, the judges should close their scorebooks in preparation for the next dive.

BASIC PENALTIES AND RULINGS

Stroke Requirements

Freestyle. Freestyle events allow the greatest freedom because any stroke or combination of strokes may be used. Any part of the body may touch the wall in executing a turn while the finish may be made by touching the wall with either hand.

Breaststroke. The breaststroke event calls for the swimmer to remain on the surface with a portion of his head above the water except after the final arm-pull prior to a turn or the finish. The hands must be moved forward and backward simultaneously and the feet must kick in an outward sweep to the rear. Only one full stroke and kick may be executed underwater on the turns. The touch must be made with both hands simultaneously. The most common infractions include the head going underwater on the stroke and dolphin-kicking off the wall. The major consideration in disqualification should be: Is he swimming on top of the water?

Butterfly.   In the butterfly, the hands must be recovered out of the water. The undulation of the legs and feet in the kick call for simultaneous and symmetrical movements. The touch is the same as that of the breaststroke. Infractions are most commonly called for breaking the legs apart in the dolphin kick.

Backstroke.   The swimmer must remain on his back, including touches, during the course of the race. A hand touch is required at each turn and the swimmer's hips may not turn over beyond the vertical before his foremost hand has touched the end of the pool.[3]

TABLE 6.1
Meet Scoring

	Dual Meet	Championship Meet
Individual Events	5-3-1-0	7-5-4-3-2-1
Relays	7-0	14-10-8-6-4-2-1

TABLE 6.2
Diving Scoring

Very Good	8.5-10
Good	6.5- 8
Satisfactory	5.0- 6.0
Deficient	2.5- 4.5
Unsatisfactory	0.5- 2.0
Completely Failed	0

PROBLEM CALLS

Close Finishes
Due to the closeness of many races, the finish position becomes all important. Judges must secure an advantageous station along the finish to render a sound decision. It is hoped that electronic timing devices will solve this problem in the near future. New facilities undoubtedly enjoy this luxury while administrators, athletic directors and coaches of older facilities must plead their cases with budget authorities in order to become equipped with such systems. The common problems of splashing and underwater touches emphasize the need for electronic devices, especially in freestyle and backstroke finishes. Many coaches actually encourage their swimmers to raise their heads and make a splash prior to touching the wall in a close finish.

3. *Ibid.,* p. SW-15.

Rolling Starts

A legal start requires all contestants to attain their starting positions, remain motionless and wait for the starting gun. A rolling start is one which swimmers persist in slow downward movement in assuming their starting positions. Consequently, there is considerable motion. This motion exists both in the normal hang starting positions and the grab starting cantilevered positions. When a swimmer or swimmers are moving, the "Stand up" command should be used to obviate the need for calling a false start. When this is not possible, a false start must be charged to the swimmer committing the infraction. Starters must be firm in their efforts to assure an equitable start for all contestants. From age group swimming through university competition, starters must work for consistency. The commands should be varied in timing and given in a calm, quiet voice to avoid exciting the swimmers and promoting false starts.

FIG. 6.7
Normal Start

FIG. 6.8
Grab Start

Relay Take-offs

The most common infraction may be the relay take-off. Take-offs are difficult to judge since many touches are made underwater. Volunteer judges hesitate to make such an instrumental call. If the starter is working the meet alone, he cannot judge the touch and take-off from a distance with any confidence. Championship meets, with an adequate number of officials, have a take-off judge assigned to each lane. The advent of automatic timing devices should minimize this problem.

Stroke Infractions

Stroke infractions must be declared without delay to the referee in keeping with the rules. Swimmers shown leniency, regardless of age, are permitted an unfair advantage and fail to demonstrate a competitive skill. Stroke infractions should be strictly enforced in age group swimming, closely observed in high school swimming and almost nonexistent in college swimming. It might be a good policy to develop hand signals for stroke inspectors for agreement on stroke infractions leading to disqualification. Stroke technique is best observed from behind the swimmers.

Volunteer Officials

In order to conduct an organized swimming meet, several officials are required. Championship meets require as many as thirty officials. Due to financial circumstances, it is usually not feasible to have a full complement of officials for dual meets. Consequently, many of these responsibilities are assigned to volunteer officials. This creates a situation in which the host school or club must secure the services of interested individuals. It is necessary that either a clinic be conducted prior to the meet date or a premeet meeting should be staged well before the scheduled hour of the meet. This session should explain how to use a watch, positioning at the start and the finish of the race, recording procedures and many other details. Prominent meet directors recognize the importance of these volunteers and make it a point to keep them well informed. Basic instructions should be attached to each official's clipboard. If a banquet is customary at the conclusion of the season, it is beneficial to the program to invite the volunteer officials as a way of recognizing them.

OFFICIATING EVALUATED BY COACHES

What qualities do you appreciate in a swimming official?

PETER DALAND—University of Southern California:

> Promptness, decisiveness, knowledge of the rules, willingness to make the necessary disqualifications and neatness.

CHARLES ARNOLD—University of New Hampshire:

> One who is completely familiar with the rules and applies them equally in all situations.

RICHARD PAPENGUTH—Purdue University:

> One who gives confidence to the athletes.

What qualities do you dislike in a swimming official?

BILL CAMPBELL—University of Maryland:

> Egotism, poor voice, know-it-allness and tardiness.

PHIL MORIARTY—Yale University:

Carelessness, timid, disinterested and influenced by crowd reaction.

JOHN H. HIGGINS—United States Naval Academy:

The official that feels that he has not had a good day unless he disqualifies one or two athletes.

Miscellaneous comment

AL MALTHANER—Principia College:

The officials should take command of the contest without calling undue attention to themselves. They should arrive equipped with guns, whistles, proper uniforms, rules book (for reference to a doubting coach), and keep active in officials' organizations.

OFFICIATING EVALUATED BY OFFICIALS

What is the most difficult situation to call in swimming?

CHARLES BUTT—Bowdoin College, Chairman, NCAA Swimming Rules Committee:

Difficult to truly observe the end of the races due to water splashing—rules not clearly defined on legal strokes (breaststroke).

RICHARD PAPENGUTH—Purdue University:

Finishes of close races and situations where timers and finish judges disagree.

DON GAMBRIL—Harvard University, Assistant Coach, 1968 Olympic Swimming Team:

Don't disqualify on guesswork. You must see the violation and be certain of it.

MONTE NITZKOWSKI—Long Beach City College, Head Coach, 1972 Olympic Water Polo Team:

Relay starts and finishes without electronic timing devices—the fact that it only happens once does not allow you a second look.

JACK ROWAN—Coaches and Officials Association of Southern California:

In swimming, it has to be the kick (frog kick) in the breaststroke. Most swimmers dolphin some, coming off the wall, making it a matter of opinion as to how much advantage the swimmer has gained. Has the swimmer gained enough of an advantage to be disqualified?

What is the most difficult phase of mechanics in officiating swimming?

ROBERT L. CLOTWORTHY—Princeton University:

Relay takeoffs are difficult to judge.

JAMES A. GAUGHRAN—Stanford University:

The starter's command should be made in a way which doesn't invite false starts. Inflection in voice should fall rather than raise on a starting command.

DUANE L. DRAVES—Coaches and Officials Association of Southern California:

The official is on the deck which quite often is not high enough to observe the full field of competitors at the finish.

Miscellaneous comment

AL ZAMSKY—College of Dupage:

One of the biggest problems that I find, which often affects many sports, is the problem of the official not being involved in public education or a coach who forgets he is involved with public education. In brief, officials often display unprofessional conduct in speech, dress or mannerisms. In few sports is a coach, an official or players allowed conduct which would be considered offensive to the public. It would seem that some coaches and officials forget this and act as if their job and life depended on that game.

MISCELLANEOUS CONSIDERATIONS

Automatic Timing Devices

A completely automatic device is one which automatically starts with the starter's pistol and stops when a contestant touches the finish contact pad. A semiautomatic device automatically starts with the starter's pistol or manually and stops when the lane judge presses a button when the swimmer in his assigned lane finishes. Timing equipment must not interfere with the swimmers' starts, turns, or the function of the overflow system.[4] In case of a malfunction, lane judges and timers must be utilized in the ballot system.

BIBLIOGRAPHY

National Collegiate Athletic Association. *Swimming Guide* (Phoenix: Collegiate Athletic Publishing Service, 1973.

4. *Ibid., p.* SW-12.

Chapter VII

Track and Field

THE GAME

Track and field competition is unique in that several events progress concurrently and an opportunity exists for all members of the team to compete. Due to the overlapping of events, there are understandable delays which are time consuming. With reliance on individual effort, the contestants exhibit considerable tenseness. The referee-starter, therefore, must make an attempt to calm both the competitors and coaches. As in swimming, the referee-starter is usually the only paid official. Consequently, he must supervise a corps of officials.

OFFICIALS AND THEIR RESPONSIBILITIES

Referee and Starter

The referee is responsible for ensuring fair competition for all contestants. Both the referee and the starter functions are normally performed by one official. The referee-starter is responsible for the disqualification of contestants who violate the rules. He works closely with the head timer, head judge of finish, chief inspector and the chief field judge. The starter must have an extensive knowledge of all running and field events. In running events, the starter has full control of all competitors at the start. The starter must be able to clarify the conditions for competing in each running event. On races over one-quarter mile, the starter should signal the start of the last lap of the race. The starter must have the capacity to make fast, fair and firm decisions.

FIG. 7.1
Qualifies. American runner
Reynaud Robinson of Lakeland,
Florida, comes to an easy finish during Thursday's 100-
meter track and field qualification event at the Olympic
Games in Munich—31 August
1972 (AP Wirephoto via Cable
from Munich).

Inspectors

Spaced to best observe their assigned lanes, the inspectors should
concentrate on runners changing course and impeding an opponent in his
effort to pass. They must also determine during relay races whether or
not the baton was passed in the prescribed passing zone. The chief inspector is responsible for his three assistants and for reporting violations
to the referee-starter.

Clerk of the Course

The clerk of the course has the important task of seeing that the meet
progresses according to the time schedule. He is responsible for assigning
contestants to their proper lane positions prior to each race and placing
all members of relay teams in their proper lanes.

Finish Judges

The order of finish in all races is the responsibility of the head judge of finish and his assistant judges. In dual meets, there may only be three assistant judges, one assigned to pick each place. In championship meets at least two judges should be assigned to determine each place. The head judge of finish must view each finish and be prepared to resolve any conflicts in placing as determined by the judges.

Field Judges

Each field event has a judge and several assistants. The judge of each field event is responsible for conducting each event by the rules governing that event. He is responsible for both fair and foul competition. The judge at each event is also responsible for the activities of his assistants in marking and measuring legal throws and jumps. The head field judge, in turn, supervises the overall conduct of the field events. This includes weighing, measuring and inspecting all implements, checking the order of competition, and certifying any record made during the course of the meet.

Scorer

The primary responsibility of the scorer is to maintain running team scores as the results of the events are presented to him. This should include a record of individual winners and their performances.

Announcer

Meet information should be dispensed to the contestants and spectators throughout the meet. Announcements should be kept to a minimum in order to avoid interrupting and taking attention away from the competition. It is the responsibility of the announcer to give the ten minute first call and the five minute second call for each event.

Marshall

The marshall is responsible for keeping the competitive areas clear and all unauthorized people—athletes not competing in the event in progress—off the track and infield. This practice should ensure the steady progress of the meet. The marshall should be identified by cap or a ribbon worn on his jacket.

FUNDAMENTAL SKILLS

Starting

A pistol of not less than .32 caliber, that can be cocked and has a flash that is clearly visible to the timers, must be used. The pistol should

FIG. 7.2
On Your Marks!

FIG. 7.3
Set!

be carefully inspected before each race to make sure that it is fully loaded. The starter should repeat race instructions to the participants and answer any questions that may be presented. He should then signal the head finish judge to alert him to the start of the race. After receiving a return signal from the head finish judge, the starter should take a position ten-to-fifteen-yards ahead of the competitors to the side away from the bleachers or stands. In a stagger race, the starter should position himself two-to-three-yards in front of the lead runner in lane 1 or 2, so he can observe all the runners. In a calm and relaxed voice, the starter should bring the runners to the starting line by giving the command, "On your marks!" while pointing his free hand to the ground. Allowing ample time for all contestants to get comfortable in the starting blocks, the starter should then raise his free hand over his head, in the same position as the gun hand, and give the command "Set" requesting that the participants now assume their final positions. After an interval of approximately two seconds and when all participants are motionless, the starter should discharge the pistol. If a runner or runners cause an illegal start, they must be charged with a false start.[1] Two false starts result in disqualification. As soon as the participants leave the starting line, the starter's assistants should remove the blocks to the infield. In races of 880 yards and over, the commands are "Runners, take your marks" and the gun for high school and "Runners, set" and the gun for college competition.

1. National Collegiate Athletic Association. *Track and Field Guide* (Phoenix: College Athletics Publishing Service, 1972), p. 13.

Timing

Timers should be instructed to clear their watches upon receiving the command from the head finish judge, alerting them to the start of the next race. Due to the distance to the starting line, up to 220 yards, the timers must watch for the flash or the smoke from the gun for the start. After taking the slack out of the watch, or depressing the stem until contact is made, the watch is started with the forefinger when the flash of the gun is observed. The slack should be taken out of the watch stem again as the runners approach the finish. Approximately ten yards from the finish, the timers should direct their attention to the finish line. A "torso" finish is official in track. The man who breaks the string is not necessarily the winner. The runner who reaches the finish line first, exclusive of head, arms and feet is the winner. The runner does not have to come over the finish line with entire body. After each race, the timer should show his watch to the head timer who will record the time.

Judging

Running events. Judges should position themselves at least ten yards back from the finish line, on elevated stands, on either side of the track. Following each race, the finish judge will select his man, on the basis of the torso finish. Even though the runners have been instructed to stay in their lanes and to turn around and face the judges at the end of the race, it is necessary for the judges to physically go to his man and get his name. The judge should report his selection to the head finish judge who records the official finish. If there is a conflict at the finish, the head judge should conduct a meeting to resolve the official finish order.

Field events. The head field judge, event judges and measurers should work together as a team to expedite the conduct of the field events. It is essential for each field judge to be aware of the local ground rules. The head field judge must also ascertain whether the individual field judges have the necessary equipment to conduct the event. Along with the event scorecard, an instruction card that clearly outlines the basic rules of the event, should be attached to the clipboard. Figure 7.4 is an example of the instruction card. After each attempt, the judge should verify the measurement and instruct the event assistants to prepare the area for the next competitor. To expedite matters, it is suggested that the judge announce the "on deck" competitor. A rule of thumb in measurement calls for measuring to the nearest one-fourth inch under 100 feet and to the nearest inch over 100 feet. At the conclusion of the event, the judge should record the place order and turn in the results to the scorer.

Long Jump

1. Six official entries (3 attempts)
2. Four advance to the finals (3 attempts)
3. Keep scratch line clean
4. Measure from point of entry to front edge of scratch line
5. Measure at right angles from the point of entry to the front edge of the scratch line extended (jumps entering extreme sides of the pit)
6. Falling back and out of the pit to gain balance is a foul jump

FIG. 7.4
Instruction Card

BASIC PENALTIES AND RULINGS

Lane Violations

A competitor must be disqualified if he crosses over into the lane inside him and takes three or more steps before returning to his assigned lane in races around the curve. Runners may also be disqualified for jostling, cutting across, or obstructing another competitor by impeding his progress. The major concern is to note any action that causes another runner to break his stride or lose momentum. Inspectors should be cognizant of the importance of their responsibility. Too often, this assignment is taken too lightly and as a result the contestants suffer.

Relay Passes

The most important consideration is that the pass be made within the allotted zone of twenty meters, and that after making the pass, the runner does not veer out of his lane thus impeding the opponent's path. From a technical standpoint, the baton must be passed within the zone. The man may be out of the passing zone. If the baton is dropped in the passing zone, either runner may pick it up.

Hurdle Clearance

A hurdler must be disqualified if he advances or trails a leg or foot alongside a hurdle. His legs must go over the hurdle. He may also be disqualified for running out of his lane and obstructing another hurdler or deliberately knocking down hurdles.

Events Using Circles—Shot, Discus, Hammer

A foul attempt is charged for touching the top edge of the circle or the ground outside the circle. The implement must land within the prescribed sector. In the shot put, the shot must not drop behind or below the shoulder.

High Jump

An illegal jump is an attempt made from other than one foot. If the jumper falls back into the standards, thus causing the bar to fall off, the attempt is also counted as a miss. Though commonly believed, it is not true that a contestant must leave the pit before the bar falls. Regardless of when or how the bar falls, the attempt must be declared a miss.

Pole Vault

The basic factor to consider in making judgments on the pole vault is that the contestant may not move his upper hand higher on the pole or raise his lower hand above the upper hand during the vault. Released poles may be recovered by event judge assistants if they are falling back toward the judges or away from the crossbar. In successful jumps over sixteen feet, the pole may also be recovered when falling under the crossbar to avoid having the pole hit the jumper.

Long Jump

Measurements must be made at right angles from the point of entry to the front edge of the scratch board. If necessary to gain a right angle measurement, an extension of the scratch board may be made. A clipboard should suffice. See figure 7.5.

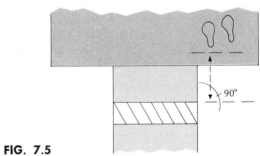

FIG. 7.5

Triple Jump

The major problem in the triple jump event is that of technique. The foot that starts the jump must hit first, followed by the opposite foot and then the jump into the pit. In a legal jump the trail foot may not touch the runway. Measurement for the triple jump is the same as that for the long jump. To avoid injury to jumpers, the landing pit should be at least thirty-six feet from the scratch board.

Scoring
Dual meet scoring for individual events is 5-3-1 for the first three places. Relays in dual meets are scored 5-0. In championship meets, scoring varies according to the number of teams entered.

PROBLEM CALLS

Event Delays
To avoid delay, it was previously suggested that the "on deck" or next competitor be announced. Contestants participating in two or more events at the same time should be encouraged to return to an event as soon as possible in order to receive their allotment of attempts. In a running event, the judge must ascertain that a reasonable recovery period be given when the competitor returns. There seems to be considerable difference of opinion as to how long the judge must wait for a contestant to return. Many judges feel that if a participant returns during the round in progress, he should go to the end of the order and then resume his original position in the next round. Regardless of the procedure adopted, the competitor should not delay the orderly progress of the event. The Track and Field Guide note on the subject is as follows:

> The Games Committee should fix a time by which all preliminaries in the long jump and triple jump shall have been completed. Whatever jumps have not been taken by this time shall be forfeited.[2]

For the same reason that one man can score in two or more events that are running simultaneously, he should be required to finish in the prescribed amount of time. This constitutes an integral part of the competition.

False Starts
False starts are sometimes the result of faulty starting techniques. Starters must be constantly aware that in short distance competition the runners are anxious and tend to anticipate. Some starters have eliminated changes in body positions in starting hand signals as runners often react to the hand being raised on the command "Set." Many times, a quiet confident manner will sufficiently relax the competitors so that they will not

2. *Ibid.*, p. 30.

try to second guess the starter. The starter must be cautious not to hurry his commands and therefore invite false starts. If the starter is not satisfied with the final running positions of the competitors in the blocks, he should request that they stand up; he should not assess a false start. To protect the best interests of all contestants, the starter must allow ample time for all runners to prepare for second start without undue hurrying.

Long Jump and Triple Jump Judging

Careful scrutiny of the toe and the end of the board, or scratch line, must be practiced to effectively judge these events. A good practice would be to clear the area immediately near the board and pit to offset the probability of contestants and spectators second guessing the judge. Foul calls should be made immediately after the contestant makes contact with the pit. If foul calls are made while the jumper is still in the air, injury to the jumper may result. This is a judgment decision that must be made quickly. Contact with the ground surface in front of the board is not always evident. The toe of the shoe may extend over the board without marking the sand, dirt or runway in front of the board in many instances. Jumpers falling back and out of the pit to regain their balance must be charged with a foul jump. The judge must also be on guard to protect the participants from nonparticipants who may be warming up near the runway.

Relay Exchanges

Too often this facet of the meet is grossly overlooked. Since meets may not be decided even at the time of the relay, indifference in judging relay exchanges could be disastrous. Inspectors must observe the passes and rule accordingly. With only one inspector on each exchange position, it is very difficult to observe all the passes accurately.

OFFICIATING EVALUATED BY COACHES

What qualities do you appreciate in a track and field official?

Dixon Farmer—University of Michigan:

> Friendliness at the same time professional attitude is demonstrated. Too few officials have the ability to combine these qualities.

N. J. Kovalakides—University of Maryland:

> 1. Thorough knowledge of the rules.
> 2. Hustles.
> 3. Demonstrates a desire to provide good officiating.
> 4. Shows up in plenty of time to start on time.

VERN COX–Springfield College:
1. Fairness—all runners afforded an equal start.
2. Personality—firm and exact but not harsh.
3. Willingness—to accept responsibility and prepare for the assignment.

DON MULLIGAN—Long Beach City College:
Goes out of his way to run a good meet . . . has courage.

DAVE KAMANSKI—Cerritos College:
Fairly quiet, goes about his job without being noticed, checks everything that is his responsibility, conscientious, calm and relaxed.

What qualities do you dislike in a track and field official?
JIM BUSH—UCLA:
A man that barks at the boys and is always hurrying them. This tends to make the boys nervous and has, in some cases, led to injuries.

PAYTON JORDAN—Stanford University:
Unsolicited coaching of athletes during competition.

JOE LANNING—Long Beach City College:
Lateness and not assuming responsibility.

Miscellaneous comments
DON RUH—Mount San Antonio College:
Good officials must remember that they are there to help the athlete. The athlete must be aware that the official is giving his time for him and thus deserves much respect.

FRANK POTTS—University of Colorado:
I think track officials need to study the rules more often and do some thinking before accepting an officiating job even if it is for no compensation.

RON MORRIS—California State University, Los Angeles:
An official must be available during the warmup period (pole vault and high jump) to aid in bar and standard placement. This gives everyone a chance to be ready at the starting height.

OFFICIATING EVALUATED BY OFFICIALS

What is the most difficult situation to call in track and field?
LEON Q. FORMAN—Southern California Track Starters' Association:
Detecting a rolling start.

ERNIE JENSEN—Southern California Track Starters' Association:
Lack of meet management—lack of officials—lack of block and hurdle crew.

What is the most difficult phase of mechanics in officiating track and field?

J. WALTER SMITH—Glendale College:

Starter's position for races run from a staggered start.

JACK NEWMAN—past president of the Southern California Track Starters' Association:

Schools do *not* have adequate finish line stands in which to properly judge the finish. Actually, in most stadiums, you get a better picture from the *stands. That is where the judges should be.*

LEON Q. FORMAN—Southern California Track Starters' Association:

Finish line when many timers and judges are present and no stands for the judges (aligning oneself with finish line).

Miscellaneous comments

JACK NEWMAN—past president of the Southern California Track Starters' Association:

It has been my experience that the head coach must be a good organizer, a devoted man to his sport, to build his physical plant and enlist proper officiating help. Unfortunately, we find that is not always the case; and, consequently, I find that at many colleges the meet lacks unity, and it drags along simply because the officials and judges are inexperienced and/or the equipment is below par. I find that I am becoming a little more "selective" when I accept an assignment as starter, working only for those schools whose meets progress smoothly.

JOHN E. KASHIWABARA, M.D.—S.P.A.A.U.:

The official with whom I like to work is one who is thoroughly familiar with the rules and regulations and one who can make decisions in "gray area" situations.

MISCELLANEOUS CONSIDERATIONS

Premeet Duties

The referee and starter should arrive early to inspect the track, starting lines, finish lines, relay passing zones and field event facilities and equipment. A meeting with both coaches should be conducted to clarify rules and answer any questions. The few minutes allotted for this meeting will usually pay dividends before the meet has ended.

Volunteer Officials

Finding reliable and capable volunteer officials is probably the most difficult phase of track coaching. Time must be devoted to the active recruiting of these volunteer officials. Experienced volunteer officials should be solicited each year and commitments secured when possible. A personal contact should be made to assure them that their services are important to the continuance of the sport. On the day of the meet, the coach should make every effort to refamiliarize these individuals regarding their responsibilities. The coach should also take time to review the instruction cards attached to each field event scorecard with his volunteer officials. Take nothing for granted; if there are rule changes, clarify these before the meet. Don't assume that even experienced volunteers have kept up-to-date on rule changes in any given event. Make provisions for questions before the meet. It is the responsibility of the coach to support these volunteers by moving around during the meet and assisting them with tact. The coach should make it a point to thank all volunteer officials at the conclusion of each meet.

BIBLIOGRAPHY

National Collegiate Athletic Association. *Track and Field Guide*. Phoenix: Collegiate Athletic Publishing Service, 1972.

Chapter VIII

Volleyball

THE GAME

From the official's point of view there are three particularly important aspects of volleyball: (1) the pace of the game is explosively fast; (2) judgment on ball handling is *the most* crucial officiating responsibility; and (3) the approach to volleyball is more amateurlike, and more sportsmanlike than in any other popular American sport.

The volleyball official, therefore, must have lightninglike reactions and very fine concentrative powers in order not to become absolutely overwhelmed by the speed of the action. He must also understand the principles underlying ball handling decisions and volleyball in general. He must exemplify at all times the fine spirit of this tremendous game; that is, he must be gentlemanly but firm; he must love the game; he must enter into his volleyball officiating with an attitude of serving the players —he must not be a tyrant nor a battle-hardened arbiter.

Two unusual items included in the *United States Volleyball Association Guide* illustrate the unique and "fresh" approach to volleyball. The USVBA encourages honor calls where players acknowledge their own infractions. There is also a special referee's hand signal to recognize good sportsmanship. The signal is the traditional sportsman's victory signal— the hands clasped over the head.

Obviously, then, volleyball officials have a key role to play—not only in enforcing the rules, but in exemplifying and supporting the sportsmanlike approach generally taken by volleyball players.

OFFICIALS AND THEIR RESPONSIBILITIES

Volleyball officials include the referee, umpire, linesman, scorer and timekeeper. According to the level of play, volleyball is or has been officiated by any number of officials from zero to eight.

Referee

The referee has final control. He may overrule any other official, although he uses considerable discretion in exercising this power. Ideally, the referee takes a position on an elevated stand or table at one end of the net so that his line of vision is well above the top of the net. He places one hand on the net cable to help detect illegal touches of the net.

The referee routinely causes the game to progress. He blows his whistle and beckons the server to put the ball in play. He again sounds

FIG. 8.1

his whistle to kill the play when a rally has ended or a foul has occurred. Finally, he awards a point, declares "side out" or orders a replay, as the case warrants. While the referee may rule on any action that occurs, he is particularly concerned about ball handling fouls, fouls at or above the net, player conduct fouls and routine matters such as granting substitutions and time-outs.

Umpire

The umpire takes a moving position at the end of the net opposite the referee. His chief responsibilities are to rule on fouls below the net and over the center line and to assist the referee with ball handling decisions, net violations and player conduct rulings. The umpire checks the duration of delays caused by time-outs, injuries, or intermission during a match.

FIG. 8.2

Before each serve the umpire should station himself several feet to the receiving team's side of the net. This will enable him to enforce positioning regulations of the receiving team. The alert and competent umpire is mobile, constantly adjusting his position near the net similar to the movement of the lead basketball official (the basketball official under the basket). Mobility reminds the players of the umpire's presence and enables him to gain a better viewing position. In recent years, competent volleyball umpires have increased both the range and speed of their movement.

While a degree of responsibility overlaps between umpire and referee, it is helpful to remember that (1) the umpire's attention is more the the "bottom half" of the action and (2) the referee's attention is more to the "top half," as well as to overall discretion and power.

Linesmen

There may be two or four linesmen. Their floor positions are (1) behind each corner of the court (four linesmen) or (2) behind two diagonally opposite corners of the court (two linesmen). They are far enough from the court to avoid obstructing player movement and close enough to view clearly the boundary lines for which they are responsible. During the game action they are concerned about three aspects of the playing rules: (1) Was the ball in or out of bounds when it struck the court? (2) Was the server in a proper position behind the end line when he served? (3) Was the ball in-bounds when it passed over the net? The linesmen employ prescribed hand signals to indicate whether a ball is on or off the court and sound their whistles—rarely—to rule on an illegal serve or a ball passing over the net out of bounds.

Scorer and Timekeeper

While the United States Volleyball Association rules place the scorer and timekeeper opposite the referee and near the umpire, some referees prefer to have them positioned on their side of the court for easy verbal communication purposes. Preferably, they are seated at a table far enough from the court so as not to impede the players' and umpire's movement. The functions of the scorer are to record the score and/or operate scoring devices, to receive the starting lineups, to keep track of proper positioning and to answer any questions that arise about such positioning, to record all time-outs and substitutions, and to verify that all players are in their proper serving order prior to the start of a game. The scorer is also empowered to sound his horn when a player is not in the proper serving position at the instant the ball is served.

The timekeeper is positioned near the scorer. He keeps a record of the time that the ball is in play in each game, starting his timing device

POSITIONS OF VOLLEYBALL OFFICIALS

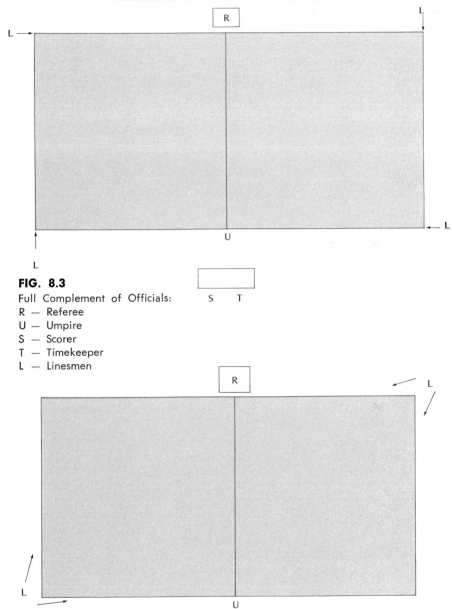

FIG. 8.3
Full Complement of Officials:
R — Referee
U — Umpire
S — Scorer
T — Timekeeper
L — Linesmen

FIG. 8.4
A Common Tournament Compromise:
R — Referee
U — Umpire
L — Linesmen

when each serve is contacted and stopping it when the ball becomes dead or a whistle sounds. He sounds his horn when the eight minute playing time of a game has expired. If the remaining time is not visible to the players near the end of the period, he is instructed to call out the remaining time in a loud voice.

FUNDAMENTAL SKILLS

"Movement with the play" is extremely difficult in volleyball because of the quickness of the action within a restricted playing area. The solution to the need for good positioning in volleyball is to place the referee, the umpire and the linesman in relatively stable positions surrounding the playing area. From these semi-stationary positions, their intent is not to move with the action, but to concentrate upon vision of the ball and the action—action which at times is probably faster than in any other sport.

Thus, mechanics and fundamental skills are largely limited to the use of the whistle and hand signals, teamwork with other officials and certain game routines which are peculiar to volleyball.

Use of the Whistle

The referee's whistle controls all volleyball action. It tells the server when he must serve and it sounds the end of a rally, killing the play. The umpire's whistle can also kill the play for cause. A well officiated volleyball match is characterized by frequent, considered and definite hand signals and whistle soundings, *not* by verbal communication among officials, players and coaches.

There is an art to the use of the whistle in volleyball. The experienced and capable volleyball official varies his use of the whistle according to the circumstances. When the action is fast and hectic, it is sometimes necessary for him to sound his whistle repeatedly with short, sharp blasts. Occasionally, when a ball is clearly out of bounds, only the mildest whistle is needed. The same is true when a serve is hit into the net. The referee's whistle directing the server to serve should be of diminished intensity—just loud enough to gain the attention of all players, but no louder. New officials are cautioned to hold their whistles out of their mouths when conversing with players, coaches or other officials.

Hand Signals

Decisive and clear hand signals are very important to the success of a volleyball official. Good hand signals tend to eliminate the necessity for unneeded verbal communication and excessive use of the whistle. When whistling can be reduced, the game becomes more the *player's* game rather than the official's game.

There are three requisites to effective hand signaling in volleyball. First, *know all the signals*, so that each can be used appropriately; second, execute the signals decisively, yet not dictatorially; and third, choose the right moment to exercise the signal, so that it need not be repeated or explained. There is an exact moment when all players and spectators normally look to the referee or umpire—whoever sounded the whistle.

Teamwork Amongst Officials

As mentioned before, the referee has the authority in volleyball to overrule another official. Obviously, this authority should be exercised with discretion. Players and coaches, not to mention the other officials, become confused and irritated if the referee overrules his fellow officials too frequently or without apparent reason.

A pregame discussion among each team of officials can serve to establish the proper understanding for the particular match to be officiated. In a national or international match where the umpire and linesmen, as well as the referee are experienced and knowledgeable, very few cases of overrulings by the referee would be expected. On the other hand, at lower levels of volleyball competition, the referee is often the only member of the crew who really knows and understands volleyball rules and mechanics. In such circumstances, it is necessary for the more experienced person not only to step in when necessary, but to set the stage for this before the match. Generally, the referee should avoid overruling any decision by another official especially if he knows that the other official had a good view and knew the rule. Specifically, the referee should use extreme discretion in overruling the umpire on ball-handling decisions and under-the-net fouls.

Beyond the "referee may overrule" aspect of volleyball officials' teamwork lies the other normal aspects of officiating teamwork: a willingness to communicate with one another, a general attitude of support for one another, a collective capability to rule and signal decisively, and so forth. The relative lack of movement by volleyball officials, however, eliminates much of the necessity for teamwork found in such sports as basketball, football, baseball and water polo. One other important aspect of volleyball officiating teamwork involves a close check between the referee and the scorer and the referee and the timekeeper to ascertain that no errors have been made in either scoring or timing.

BASIC PENALTIES AND RULINGS

Scoring

A volleyball game is played to 15 points, with a two point spread needed to win, or to 8 minutes of ball in play, whichever occurs first. A match consists of two of three or three of five games. Only the serving team can score a point. If the servers' opponents win a given "point," it is termed "side out" and the serve goes to the other team. When a serve touches the net, it is a side out. After the serve, each team may touch the ball no more than three times in returning the ball to their opponents. A single player may not play the ball twice consecutively, with the exceptions of (1) the block and (2) simultaneous contact by teammates or opponents.

Service

The server must be behind and to the right ten feet of the end line when he contacts the ball. A depth of at least six feet should be provided for the server. The ball may be hit from the hand or from a toss.

Fouls

No player may touch the net or step across the center line while the ball is in play. Such "violations" are disregarded, however, if they occur clearly after the referee's whistle kills the play. When the ball passes over the net, it must be within the sidelines.

Back Line Players

Back line players may not participate in blocks at the net. These players may not spike in advance of the ten foot "spiking line." Back line players may move forward of the ten foot spiking line to make a save or set the ball for a spiker.

Ball Handling

The referee should thoroughly explain his ball handling interpretations to both teams before each game and subsequently attempt to be entirely consistent in his ball handling rulings.

The ball must be struck cleanly and crisply by a body part above the waist. It may not be thrown or double-hit. Service and spike returns *must* be cleanly hit, while discretionary leniency is granted on "sets."

Miscellaneous Rulings

When any of the above rules are violated, the penalty is either side out or point for the serving team. The volleyball official's job is simplified by this uniformity of penalties (either a point or side out). There are certain special rulings, however:

1. A *game shall be forfeited* when (a) either team has fewer than six players or (b) a team refuses to play when directed to do so by the referee.
2. A *player may be disqualified* when he (a) is unsportsmanlike, (b) "persistently addresses the officials in regard to decisions," (c) employs derogatory remarks or acts towards officials or opponents, or (d) attempts to deceive officials or influence their decisions. The referee may also warn or declare a point or side out for the above acts. Disqualification is not mandatory.
3. *The points* made by a team *may be cancelled* (a) during the time when a player was serving out of turn, (b) during the time of play by a player who has entered a game for the fourth time—a player may enter the game no more than three times—or (c) during the time of play by a player who has reentered the game in a position different from his first position in the game. (Fourth-entry players and wrong-position reentry players may not remain in the game.)

One additional ruling is available to the volleyball referee. He may rule a "play-over" when the circumstances warrant. Some such circumstances are: double fouls, an official's mistake, a foreign object entering the court, a ball "held" above the net by opponents or a serious injury. The referee is accorded great leeway in calling play-overs. For example, if the eight minute horn sounds during a rally and apparently causes a player to stop, the referee may rule a play-over under the "official's mistake" clause.

United States Volleyball Association and International Rules

Posing a problem to the volleyball officials are the inconsistencies in volleyball rule interpretations between the United States Volleyball Association and International Rules, on one hand, and among various sections of the United States on the other. Nevertheless, the United States Volleyball Association official rules are so straightforward and repetitive as to make them quite easy to understand and master by the would-be volleyball official. This is in marked contrast to the difficulties encountered by the new official in baseball, basketball and football, among other sports.

PROBLEM CALLS

Ball Handling Decisions

The most difficult aspect of volleyball officiating is to maintain consistency in decisions relative to ball handling fouls. The foundation principle for ruling on borderline ball handling situations can be stated in the form of a question: "Did the ball *visibly come to rest* on the player's body part at contact?" Experienced volleyball officials and observers have found that certain hand-ball contact positions almost guarantee that the ball *will* visibly come to rest at contact. Thus, the official should be mentally prepared to signal a ball handling foul when:

1. The ball contacts the fingers and the hand in an underhand position, whether the player is facing the net or away from it.
2. Two hands are used to "throw" the ball from one side of the player's head to the other.
3. A player attempts to return a hard driven spike or serve by means of the normal two-handed overhand volleyball pass.

The three contact positions outlined above are almost always fouls. The principle of ball handling fouls, however, takes precedence. Each ball handling decision made by the great volleyball referee results from his *judgment* about whether or not the *ball visibly came to rest.*

A recent trend in volleyball officiating, caused primarily by the international volleyball influence, is for the referee to be quite strict in whistling down sloppy ball handling used in returning a hard drive spike or serve, but to be somewhat "loose" in ruling on ball handling errors occurring on the second touch by a team. (The second touch is usually referred to as the "set-up" touch.) There is considerable worldwide disagreement regarding the strictness of interpretation on third touches, or the "attacking" touch. Because of this disagreement, volleyball players are entitled to know before the start of the match just what the referee's intentions are with regard to ball handling. No other single interpretation will influence the course of a game more.

Counting Touches at the Net

The basic rules on touches are that each team is entitled to just three (and no more) touches of the ball each time a ball in play comes to their side of the net and that one player may not touch the ball twice in succession. Unfortunately, the combination of specific volleyball rule interpretations and the rapidity of play creates difficulties.

Consider the following United States Volleyball Association interpretations and you will realize more clearly how alert volleyball officials must be, especially when the action is rapid and explosive.

1. A simultaneous touch by two opponents over the net counts as *no hits* for either team.
2. The simultaneous or nearly simultaneous touches of two *or more* teammates while blocking a hard driven spike counts as *only one hit,* as long as such touches are part of a single action.

3. After the occurrence of action as described in number 2, any of the blockers may legally execute the next touch of the ball.
4. It is legal and counts as *one touch* when a player has a hard driven spike contact him twice or more in succession, as long as his action is a part of only one attempt to play the ball.

The referee who works advanced levels of volleyball action is challenged by the fact that these four touch rule extensions are *not uncommon*. Furthermore, occasionally they occur *in combination with each other* as a part of a single game action. Further complicating such situations, when they exist close to the net are the possibilities of net violations or center line violations. All of these complications can cause the referee and umpire to divide their attention and perhaps to miss an act that calls for a decision. The referee and umpire must concentrate on their individual responsibilities at the net. In particular, the referee should *concentrate primarily on the ball* and utilize his peripheral vision and feel of the net to determine whether or not other violations have occurred.

Reaching Over the Net to Block

Players may reach over the net to their opponent's side while blocking an attacking touch, but they may not block a set. A third touch may always be blocked on either side of the net. First or second touches are subject to a degree of interpretation and if there is doubt, it is better for the referee to assume that these touches were *not* attacking touches and rule against the blocker. Fortunately, experienced players rarely reach over the net to block a first or second touch, except when the ball is above the net.

Determining Net Violations

It is frequently very difficult for the referee or umpire to determine whether or not the net has been touched while the ball is in play. When from two to six opposing players are very close to the net and the action is explosive, net violations can easily be missed or ruled against the wrong team. A further complicating factor is that no net violation may be called if the *force of the ball* causes the net to brush a player.

The outstanding volleyball official has the capability, developed through years of experience, to apply direct vision to the ball and amazingly discriminating peripheral vision to the net zone. The learning official on the other hand, must rely more on his feel of the net and must supplement the feel with a constantly shifting direct vision until such time as his peripheral vision becomes more discriminating and reliable. The referee's hand-feel of the net cable can serve as a check, but there is no substitute for actually seeing the contact with the net. Volleyball officials must avoid the temptation to "guess" on net contact fouls and call only those net fouls about which they are certain.

Balls Passing Over the Net from Out of Bounds

Volleyball rules stipulate that it is a foul if the ball passes over the net out of bounds; it must be in-bounds at the moment it passes from one side of the net to the other. Unfortunately, the prescribed positions of volleyball officials make this decision a difficult one, especially when there are only two linesmen. Official rules imply that the linesmen should call such fouls. In actual practice, the referee and umpire also call them frequently even though their angle is bad.

There is no problem when these shots are directed precisely at a linesman behind one of the corners of the court. He can see it all the way. The best solution to this problem call is anticipation on the part of the linesmen—a readiness to move to the precise spot where they will have a perfect angle. A linesman is "free" to anticipate this problem call and to drastically alter his court position when the second touch is miss-directed out of bounds. The referee should instruct linesmen about this difficult decision before the game and urge them to anticipate and to move. If, during the contest the linesmen *are* anticipating and gaining good position, the referee and umpire should leave this call to the linesmen as much as possible.

Officials' View of Action Is Screened by Players

Quite often the referee or umpire is unable to see the actual touch of the ball at the precise moment of the touch because the player's back is to the official. Fortunately, either the referee or the umpire usually has an unobstructed view when his fellow official is screened. Two guidelines apply to such situations: (1) the proven officiating maxim that *you must call only what you see, not what you imagine had happened,* and (2) the referee and the umpire should accept the fact that occasionally they will be screened out and the call must be made by the other official. On such an occasion, a predetermined gesture can be used whereby one official can communicate to the other, "I was screened out—that is your call to make."

OFFICIALS EVALUATED BY COACHES

What qualities do you appreciate in a volleyball official?

Dr. Norman Kunde—University of Washington:

> One who engenders confidence as a result of demonstrating knowledge of the rules and calls violations without delay and with a suggestion of firmness.

E. B. De Groot—Santa Monica City College:

Commanding presence, imperturbable under pressure, friendliness toward players and the utilization of other officials in questionable decisions.

Dick Hammer—United States Olympic Team, 1964:

1. Consistency, promptness, command of rules and regulations.
2. Controlling—but not dominating—the game.
3. Unaffected by talk—not easily rattled.
4. Staying abreast of each play—good use of assistants.

Smitty Duke—University of Dallas:

Businesslike, no-nonsense attitude.

Kenneth E. Gongoll—Kenneth Allen Volleyball Club, Chicago:

Conducted himself so that neither the players nor the spectators noticed him and did not distract players by unnecessary actions or delays of the game.

Harry Wilson—University of California, Los Angeles:

Confidence gained through experience.

What qualities do you dislike in a volleyball official?

E. B. De Groot—Santa Monica City College:

Indecision, slow whistle and allowing players to argue with him.

Dr. Norman Kunde—University of Washington:

Not sure of rules, delay in calls and objectionable attitude.

Allen Scates—University of California, Los Angeles:

Concentration swayed by fans and does not work well with other officials.

Harry Wilson—University of California, Los Angeles:

Stylized officiating not in keeping with the written rule.

Miscellaneous comments

Will Peck—Executive Director, Grand Central YMCA, New York City:

Inconsistency on the part of a referee will drive a coach out of his mind. A coach looks for an official who possesses a high tolerance for stress and pressure.

Smitty Duke—University of Dallas:

It is very important for an official to call what he sees, not what he thinks he sees or hears. He must exhibit a professional attitude on the referee's stand. A referee should be able to make a quick decision (fair) so play is not slowed down.

E. B. De Groot—Santa Monica City College:

Volleyball officials must be cognizant not only of the rules as written, but also the *current interpretations* of the rules which change from year to year.

Mark W. Watson—Ohio Central YMCA, Columbus:

> An official can do much to transfer or build the true excitement of the game. By decisive calls and demonstrative signals, he can link the play on the floor to the observing spectators. A good official with a degree of showmanship and a fine personality can convey to the crowd moments of finesse, daring and explosiveness. His personality and his ability to control the game without being aloof and withdrawn from the players can do much to expose the nature of volleyball, which makes it a fine spectator sport. Nothing distracts from the play like the following:
>
> 1. Players asking the referee what was the call.
> 2. Players arguing with a referee who has withdrawn from the question.
> 3. Referees who allow a question to become a debate.
>
> Is it not exciting to see a referee stay with an exciting play to its termination with an equally well executed end-of-the-play signal?

OFFICIATING EVALUATED BY OFFICIALS

What is the most difficult play to call in volleyball?

Tom Leaming—United States Volleyball Association Official:

> Being able to watch a spiked ball touch blockers.

Don Shondell—United States Volleyball Association Official:

> Ball handling violations of the spike and the overhand pass, touching of the net or ball by spikers and blockers.

E. B. De Groot—United States Volleyball Association Official:

> Interpretation of the rules pertaining to ball handling or what constitutes a "held ball" or "throw."

What is the most difficult phase of mechanics in officiating volleyball?

Tom Leaming—United States Volleyball Association Official:

> Most officials' stands are not high enough to allow full view of the total play.

Harold M. Prugh—United States Volleyball Association Official:

> Making sure the hand is on the cable to see if you feel a ball hitting the net or a player contacting the net. You must make sure that you are 2 to 3 feet above the net and that you do not take your eyes off the net too soon after the spike.

Allen Scates—Commissioner of Southern California Intercollegiate Volleyball Association:

> To watch the contact directly above the net and quickly follow the flight of the ball after ascertaining that there were no infractions at the net.

Harry Wilson—United States Volleyball Association Official:

> Player's back to officials when playing the ball blocking vision of the official.

Miscellaneous comments

Will Peck—Former Chairman of Officials, United States Volleyball Association:

Volleyball requires that the official make a decision on every contact of the ball. There is little time for decision making. They must be made rapidly and accurately. A quick reaction time and a keen sense of the game is required.

Allen Scates—Commissioner of Southern California Intercollegiate Volleyball Association:

Recruiting competent officials is a definite problem in volleyball officiating. Most of the better officials are players who must maintain their amateur standing. They are not willing to work long tournaments without pay. Most of the officials have lost contact with the modern game of power volleyball.

Jerry L. McManama—United States Volleyball Association Official:

There is a definite need for more volleyball officials, especially with the recent acceptance of volleyball as a competitive sport by the N.A.I.A. and the N.C.A.A. There is a need for more volleyball officials associations.

Will Peck—Former Chairman of Officials, United States Volleyball Association:

As one who has refereed a number of sports (i.e., basketball, baseball, lacrosse and football) I would judge that volleyball officiating is more difficult since it requires that he make a judgment each time the ball is contacted by a player. There is little time for relaxing. The pressure of the official mounts as the game reaches its climax. This is when a referee must be at his best. No good volleyball referee will choke-up when the game gets tight. His calls will be at a similar level of consistency throughout the game.

E. M. Waller—United States Olympic Volleyball Committee:

As with basketball and other judgment requiring sports, the variation in officiating in various parts of the country makes it difficult for visitors at times. This is not as great a problem now because of air travel and the officiating tends to become more similar.

M. L. Walters—United States Volleyball Association Official:

The pendulum has swung in volleyball from the extreme some years ago of whistling almost every touch, to now letting the ball be literally thrown or pushed in many contests.

MISCELLANEOUS CONSIDERATIONS

Variations in Rule Interpretations

While the United States Volleyball Association has continually strengthened its position in the United States during the past two decades, the influence of international competition still has its effect upon current rule interpretations. Fortunately, the differences have been narrowed, in part by United States Volleyball Association efforts and also through expanded international competition, especially the Olympic Games. The slight differences that remain show that: (1) international interpretations are more lenient on ball handling and fouls committed in passing shots and (2) international interpretations place all of the officials in a strong no-nonsense position—not just the referee.

Lack of Qualified Volleyball Officials

The considerable upsurge of volleyball popularity in the United States has recently produced as a by-product a serious problem—a distinct shortage of qualified volleyball officials. As the quality of competition improves, the need for highly qualified officials is magnified. The players would serve as the best officials but most of them wish to preserve their amateur standing or are not interested in officiating, or both.

If the great sport of volleyball is to develop to its fullest in the United States, as it should, adequate means of producing qualified officials must be developed. At the more advanced levels of play, good officiating is absolutely essential. The game cannot be played at its best without excellent judgment on ball handling and other difficult judgment areas and without poised, intelligent and gentlemanly officiating.

Pregame Conferences

Two types of pregame conferences involving the officials are desirable before volleyball matches. First, as mentioned under "mechanics," it is necessary for the officials themselves to discuss their particular approach to the match. At this meeting such items as hand signals, use of the whistle and helping each other when screened can be reviewed; questions on particular rules and rule interpretations can be raised, analyzed and agreed upon. The emphasis in these pregame officials' conferences is upon establishing teamwork and consistency within the officiating crew. The referee should take the lead, but, according to the dictates of his personal approach, should involve each member of his crew in the discussion.

The second and unique-to-volleyball prematch conference involves the referee and the players of both teams. This traditional conference takes place on the court just before the start of the match. The referee explains to the players the interpretations, especially on ball handling, agreed upon by the officials. He asks the players for questions on the rules or on interpretations of the rules. He attempts to establish the proper rapport with the players and to build their confidence in him. He demonstrates to them that he knows the game and the rules, that he is a *gentleman* who wants the players to have a good match and that he means business and intends to enforce the rules. The pattern for a fine match can be established *before the match* through an effective referee-players pregame conference.

BIBLIOGRAPHY

United States Volleyball Association. *Volleyball Official Guide*. Berne, Indiana: United States Volleyball Association, 1972.

Chapter IX

Water Polo

THE GAME

The unique aspect of water polo is that the major part of the action takes place underwater, or out of sight. Consequently, there are numerous difficult judgment decisions for the officials working the game from the deck. It should be noted that the quality officials have had playing experience.

OFFICIALS AND THEIR RESPONSIBILITIES

The full complement of officials includes two referees, a timekeeper, two goal judges and a scorer. Financial circumstances cause many games to be played with two paid officials who assume the responsibility of both referee and goal judge.

Referees

The referees have absolute control of the game. One is designated as head referee. These officials should start and stop the game, determine when goals are scored, make decisions on goal throws, corner throws, penalty throws and penalize infractions of the rules. The head referee has final authority, and should exercise complete control over the timekeeper and the scorer. The referee is responsible for examining players of both teams for dangerous personal wear, sharp toenails and fingernails and body oils for safety reasons.

Timekeeper

The timekeeper is responsible for keeping the game clock and indicating the end of each period by sounding a pistol or clock buzzer. The

FIG. 9.1

U.S. Scores. Yugoslav Goalie Karlo Stipanic at left side of net fails to stop one of the five goals the U.S. water polo team scored against Yugoslavia Thursday at Olympic Games in Munich. Final score was 5 to 3. Players are Gary Sheerer (foreground) of Menlo Park, California, and three Yugoslav players in black headgear— 1 September 1972 (AP Wirephoto via Cable from Munich).

timer must record playing time by observing the referee's signals for ball in and out of play. College rules require a 45 second clock. The offensive team must make an attempt to shoot at their opponent's goal within 45 seconds or lose possession of the ball. This time should be kept on a stop watch. This is an effort to curb stalling techniques.

Goal Judges

The goal judges should assist the referees in signaling goal throws, corner throws, goals scored and indicating the readiness of both teams for the beginning of each period.

Scorer

The scorer maintains a record of participating players, goals scored, individual and team fouls and official time-outs. When a player receipts for his fifth personal foul, the scorer must notify the referee of his disqualification by sounding a horn loud enough to be heard by officials and coaches. The same procedure will occur when a team has accrued eight personal fouls for high school and ten personal fouls for college. This should result in a penalty throw situation for the opposing team.

MECHANICS

The two referees work opposite each other and have major responsibility to their right, as in basketball. This would include the goal area to the referee's right when the ball is in his attacking zone and a mid-pool position trailing the play when the ball is in the attacking zone at the other end of the pool. See Figure 9.2.

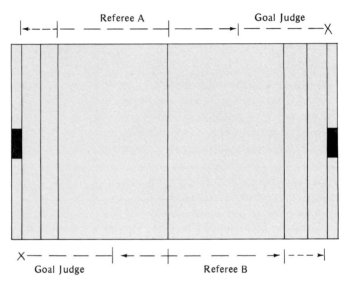

FIG. 9.2

Division of the Pool

The mechanics of officiating water polo closely parallel those used in basketball. Movement must insure full coverage of the pool area to offset one of the most common fouls in water polo, the foul away from the ball.

Positions at the Start of the Game

Players must take positions, at least one yard apart, grasping the ends of the pool on either side of the goal they are defending. The official should start play by sounding his whistle and throwing the ball into the center of the pool. Depending upon which team gains possession, the officials assume their positions moving to their right. It is important that the officials do not get caught "napping" at mid-pool when the ball is moved into the attacking zone. The referees' positions at the start of the game are shown in Figure 9.3.

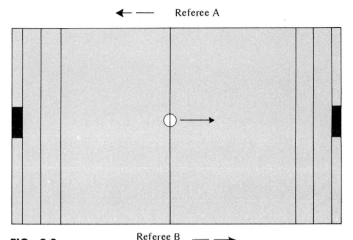

FIG. 9.3

Referee B — ⟶

Positions at the Start of the Game

Positions for a Goal Throw

If the ball is thrown past the end line, the referee will designate a goal throw to the defending goalee. The goalee must make the throw within five seconds after the referee's signal. The trailing referee should stay with the goalkeeper and the leading referee should move down the other side of the pool as shown in Figure 9.4.

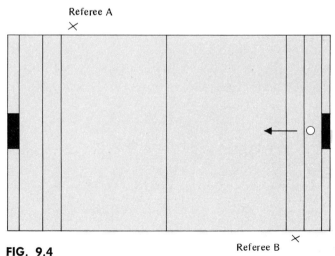

FIG. 9.4

Referee B

Positions for a Goal Throw

Positions for a Corner Throw

If the ball is deflected by the defending team and passes the goal line out of play, the attacking team should put the ball into play from the two-yard line corner on the side where the ball went out of bounds. The ball must be put into play within five seconds.

Positions for a Penalty Throw

A penalty throw must be awarded if an attacking player is fouled within the four-yard line or if a team has incurred eight or ten fouls respectively for a high school or college contest. The referee should throw the ball to the offended player who is positioned on the four-yard line directly in front of the goal and give the command "Ball up." When the

FIG. 9.5
Penalty Throw Situation

thrower has the ball up and ready for the attempt, a second whistle should be sounded for the penalty throw. The player must immediately throw the ball at the goal.

FUNDAMENTAL SKILLS

Whistle Use

A very definite, strong, clear and workable whistle is needed to keep the players alert to game situations. The whistle should be kept in the mouth at all times, except when speaking. It should be sounded in short, loud blasts and continued if not heard.

Penalty Flag Use

The home team must supply the two referees and two goal judges with flags corresponding to the cap colors.[1] Fouls are indicated by raising the penalty flag showing the team color awarded the free throw. The other hand should point to the player who will make the free throw.

FIG. 9.6
Penalty Flag

On personal fouls, the referee should also call out the number of the offending player for the scorer. If the foul is called on the side away from the scoring table, the number should be relayed by the official on the scorer's side of the pool.

BASIC PENALTIES AND RULINGS

The categories of fouls and examples of each should be distinct in the mind of every official. They involve technical, personal, major, team and double fouls.

1. National Collegiate Athletic Association. *Official Water Polo Rules* (Phoenix: Collegiate Athletic Publishing Service, 1972), p. 7.

Free Throw

In a free throw situation, two players on the offensive team must touch the ball before a goal can be scored.

Technical Fouls

Technical fouls are noncontact fouls that are penalized with a free throw awarded to the nearest opponent in the area where the foul occurred. The most common technical fouls are as follows:

1. Starting before the whistle.
2. Holding on to the goal posts.
3. Standing on the bottom of the pool.
4. Holding the ball underwater.
5. Striking the ball with your fist.
6. Delaying the game.

Personal Fouls

Personal fouls are contact fouls penalized with a free throw. Players committing five fouls must be removed from the game. The most common personal fouls are as follows:

1. Holding, sinking or pulling back an opponent who is not holding the ball.
2. Kicking or striking an opponent with or without the ball.
3. Pushing off from or retarding the free limb of an opponent, or impeding him in any way, unless he is holding the ball.
4. Deliberately splashing water in the face of an opponent.
5. Committing any technical foul for the purpose of scoring or preventing the scoring of a goal.

Major Fouls

A major foul is a flagrant foul to be penalized with a free throw to the nearest or fouled opponent, with the offending player removed from the game. The most common major fouls are as follows:

1. Attacking, striking or kicking an opponent.
2. Refusing obedience to the referee or exhibiting unsportsmanlike conduct.
3. Deliberately interfering with the taking of a free throw, penalty throw, corner throw or goal throw.
4. Committing any additional major foul after a major or fifth personal foul.

Team Fouls

A penalty throw is awarded for the tenth personal or major foul charged against a team in college competition and the eighth personal or major foul in high school competition. Any player on the opposing team, in the pool at that time, may attempt the penalty throw. Large counting cards should be supplied by the home team. As the fouls are assessed, the number of the foul should be visible to the players and the spectators.

Double Fouls

Simultaneous fouls charged to opponents should result in a faceoff. Similar to a jump ball in basketball, the ball must be thrown into the water between two players, one for each team who have equal opportunity to play it after it has touched the water. An example would be opponents holding each other in an attempt to gain possession of the ball.[2]

PROBLEM CALLS

Faking

The problem of faking is widespread. If officials call *only* what they see, this problem will be minimized. The complexion of the game can be severely affected by such acts of anticipation. An example of faking might be a quick downward movement accompanied by a groan bringing the attention of the official to the opponent in the immediate area.

Taking Advantage of the Officials

Intimidation of officials is a popular practice in water polo. It can be offset by being technically sound in the knowledge of the rules, mechanics and basic skills. The tenor and tempo of the game is normally established early in the game. If the official demonstrates that he is in full control of the game at the outset, he should gain the confidence of the players and coaches and the game would be played according to the rules.

Contact Responsibility

As in basketball, the Tower philosophy applies again. In brief, the player who by an illegal act has placed his opponent at a disadvantage must be penalized. The referee must observe the actions of both players before rendering a decision. Generally, do not allow the defense to take the play away from the offense. Make an effort to protect the man with the ball rather than overreacting to play away from the ball. Ask yourself

2. Ibid., p. 20.

the question, "What caused the man to go underwater?" Do not speculate in situations where the water refraction may allow for only 50 percent visibility.

Free Throw on the 2 Yard Line

The rule states that there must not be any interference on the free throw. Interference may be construed as any action that involves body contact or hindering during a normal free throw. Leniency allowed the defense puts the offense at a disadvantage and encourages further violations of the rules.

Advantage to the Defending Team

The referee may refrain from calling a foul if, in his opinion, the decision would be to the advantage of the defending team. An example might be an intentional foul, at the other end of the pool, to distract from an advantage situation for the offense in the goal area.

Altering Decisions

The referee may alter any of his decisions, provided that this is done before the ball is put into play again. When an incorrect flag is signaled, play must be stopped. The ball should be called out of the water and handled by the referee prior to play being resumed. Officials working in close cooperation should rectify such mistakes. Clarification of such a call should be explained to both players and coaches. In summary, if there are any questions, stop play and call the ball out of the water.

OFFICIATING EVALUATED BY COACHES

What qualities do you appreciate in a water polo official?

R. E. KROON—El Camino College:

Obscurity, efficiency, knows rules and applies them accordingly.

NORT THORNTON—Foothill College:

Prompt, consistent, forceful and in complete control.

What qualities do you dislike in a water polo official?

TOM HERMSTAD—Golden West College:

Officials tend to *assume* what went on instead of being positive it did happen. Because things happen underwater, there is a problem of seeing everything.

RICHARD DONNER—San Mateo College:

1. One who consistently talks and interprets his own decisions.
2. One who fraternizes with players on one or both teams.
3. One who is not firm in his play calling.

Howie Clark—Bolsa Grande High School:

> Another undesirable quality is when the official begins to listen to the crowd and the opposing coaches and lets them get on his nerves. This type of official is never in charge of the game; he is always worried about what people are saying about him. There is no room for personal involvement of this type in the game.

Rick Rowland—University of California, Santa Barbara:

> Sarcastic attitude toward players, coaches and spectators.

Miscellaneous comments

Monte Nitzkowski—Long Beach City College, Head Coach of the 1972 United States Olympic Water Polo Team:

> There are not enough persons who have played the game. This is more important in polo officiating than in any other sport. Water polo officiating requires an artist, not a scientist.

James W. Schultz—California State University, Long Beach:

> In my opinion, water polo officiating has reached an all time low in the area of ethics, ability and sincere concern for the game. It is a tough game to officiate but not as tough and as inconsistent in applying the rules as the officials make it appear.

Tom Hermstad—Golden West College:

> My main criticism is that as the game is now called the official can influence the outcome of the game. A mistake, and they make plenty, caused most close games to be won, not by the team, but by the official. Water polo has to change or better inform its officials if the game is to remain fun and fair.

OFFICIATING EVALUATED BY OFFICIALS

What is the most difficult play to call in water polo?

Robert K. Broadway—F.I.N.A. Official, 1968 Olympic Games:

> Driving fouls and fakes.

Al Zamsky—College of Dupage:

> Inside the four with more than one man breaking to the goal.

James W. Schultz—California State University, Long Beach:

> All calls in which two participants are attempting to battle for the ball and/ or position simultaneously with neither proving a clear-cut case in point.

Ernest A. Polte—Fullerton College:

> Hole forward in control of the ball and fouls that you know are affecting play—the problem of the underwater foul that you can't see.

What is the most difficult phase of mechanics in officiating water polo?

Robert K. Broadway—F.I.N.A. Official, 1968 Olympic Games:

> Staying in your own area and keeping an overall observation of the game.

AꞏL ZAMSKY—College of Dupage:

> The communication with the table, the players, and occasionally with the coaches.

Miscellaneous comment

AꞏL ZAMSKY—College of Dupage:

> It is usually best for men to work together for quite awhile to get the feel of the other men. Older officials will work their own area and also coach for the unusual situation.

MISCELLANEOUS CONSIDERATIONS

Indecision

In situations where officials are blocked out of the play or have doubts on a particular ruling, they should not hesitate to huddle away from the players and coaches, to resolve the problem and return to play. Decisions must be definite if game control is desired.

Overcalling and Undercalling

Infractions must be penalized. However, overcalling or particular emphasis in situations not affecting play must be avoided. "Overcalling" games will often be won by the team with the greatest depth, not by the calibre of its starting team. Undercalling, on the other hand, promotes extreme physical play and may result in injury. Both extremes can be injurious to the outcome of the game.

Ejection of Star Performers

Protection of star players occurs too often. This is generally a result of advance publicity and individual matchups. This practice cannot be condoned under any circumstances. Equitable decisions must be rendered to facilitate the best interests of all players, regardless of their ability.

Standardization of the Rules

As in other sports, problems arise from players being exposed to National Collegiate Athletic Association, Amateur Athletic Union and International rules. Continuous efforts are being made to standardize the game to a point where players are not in a constant relearning process when they move from one level of competition to another.

Hints to Water Polo Officials

To improve one's ability as a referee, it is necessary to know the rules and apply them during the game. This requires practice and frequent refereeing. The need for more capable referees requires that more men with a knowledge of the game be given a chance to referee games. Following are some suggestions:

1. *Know the rules*
2. Arrive on time and be properly dressed. This includes dark glasses and/or hat when needed.
2. Use a good strong whistle (pea stone type).
4. Always be strict.
5. Do not introduce rules or pet theories of your own.
6. Never hesitate upon strict application of the rules, but do not be fanatical.
7. Be "businesslike" on the side of the pool; in other words, don't be slovenly in your actions.
8. Signal your decisions with clarity, using your flags in a positive manner.
9. Whenever a personal foul is committed, the closest referee should be sure to call out clearly the number of the offending player to the scorer, even if it is not his decision. Be sure that the scorer is notified of fouls on penalty throws and face offs resulting in a double fall.
10. Let the manner indicate that you are in charge of the match without exaggerating your own importance. Strict, *fair* and *consistent* refereeing eliminates rough play.
11. Be definite in your decisions.
12. Satisfy yourself that goal judges, scorer and timekeeper have a good knowledge of what is expected of them. Make certain that they are in the proper positions and alert.
13. Be severe in fighting and loss of temper situations.
14. Do not be influenced by spectators. Remember that supporters have a right to shout and spur their team on.
15. It is not advisable to enter into arguments with players or spectators during or immediately after a match.
16. Do not lecture the players, nor call them by name, during the match.
17. On a face off, keep nonaffected players away from the men participating in the face off (two yards away).
18. Cooperate with your partner. Cover for him when he is out of position. Don't steal his calls, but echo his whistle and reinforce his calls by pointing your flag too. Remember that only one official should follow the ball at a time.
19. Insist that coaches and spare players of opposing teams remain in their own area unless they are substituting.

20. If the official's decision causes confusion, he should call for the ball, explain his decision, and return the ball to the proper player.
21. The secret of a successful referee is *plenty of practice* and frequent studying of the rules. When off duty, always be willing to discuss and explain rules. Prior to a match, glance over the rules. It will give you confidence in application.
22. Verify team fouls and personal fouls with the scorer at the end of each quarter. Check to see that both scorebooks agree.
23. Prior to the game, see that you are familiar with the scoring procedures used at the bench and signals used for the final personal foul and team foul.[3]

BIBLIOGRAPHY

National Collegiate Athletic Association. *Official Water Polo Rules*. Phoenix: Collegiate Athletic Publishing Service, 1972.
Southern California Water Polo and Swimming Coaches Association. *Water Polo Case Book*. LaPuente: Clay Systems and Printing Company, 1968.

3. Southern California Water Polo and Swimming Coaches Association, *Water Polo Case Book* (LaPuente: Clay Systems and Printing Company, 1968), p. 26. (public domain)

Chapter X

Wrestling

THE GAME

Wrestling is unique among the sports discussed in this book as it involves man against man in physical combat. The actions of the wrestlers are quick and are accompanied by constantly changing positions. In wrestling, an official may manually or verbally warn a contestant of a potential injury situation if his whistle is not readily available. No other sport allows the coach to observe the action so closely. As in basketball, the judgment of the referee has a great influence on the outcome of the match.

OFFICIALS AND THEIR RESPONSIBILITIES

Referee

The referee has full control of the meet and his decisions are final. The referee's primary responsibilities include checking the wrestlers to avoid health and safety hazards, clarification of the rules, awarding points for competitive maneuvers, penalizing for infractions of the rules and finally for declaring a winner. The referee should be constantly alert to detect illegal holds to minimize injuries. The head timer should be instructed by the referee.

Match Timekeeper

The timekeeper is responsible for all assistants, keeping the overall time of each match, riding time, time-out for injury and calling out the time remaining in the period to the referee, combatants and spectators.

FIG. 10.1
Grappling for Gold Medal. Wayne Wells of Norman, Oklahoma, grapples with West Germany's Adolf Seger (back to camera) in the final bout of the 163-pound (74-kilos) wrestling event of the Olympic Games in Munich Thursday night. Wells defeated Seger to win the gold medal. Seger took the bronze medal—1 September 1972 (AP Wirephoto via Cable from Munich).

Scorer

The scorer should work closely with the timekeeper and record the points scored as signaled by the referee. The scorer is also responsible for recording the down positions during the course of the match. The team score is the scorer's final responsibility.

MECHANICS

The most important concern for the referee is to move constantly to secure the best possible position to observe both wrestlers. Not moving diminishes the effectiveness of the referee and encourages illegal holds and possible injury to the competitors. The referee should stay far enough away from the wrestlers to avoid blocking the view of the other officials and spectators. The referee must be alert to anticipate troublesome situa-

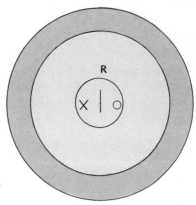

FIG. 10.2
Position at the Start of the Match

Scoring Table

tions. It must be remembered that wrestlers change positions so fast that several points may be awarded in a few seconds.

The outside position of the referee affords the best possible position to see both men and off mat limits. This position also allows the referee sufficient area to avoid exposing himself to wrestlers coming over on top of him.

While Wrestlers Are on Their Feet

The referee sounds a whistle to start the match. The official should face the scoring table with the contestants, scorers and timers in full view. The referee should keep moving from one side of the wrestlers to the other to get a clear view of both sides, keeping a safe distance to avoid interfering with the progress of the match. The referee should concern

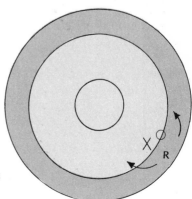

FIG. 10.3
Position for Edge of the Mat Calls

himself with wrestlers intentionally backing off the mat and stalling techniques.

While Wrestlers Are on the Mat

The referee must be alert while the wrestlers are down on the mat as positions are subject to quick changes. When the wrestlers become entangled, it is difficult to tell who has the advantage, especially along the edge of the mat. The referee should start the match in the referee's position at the beginning of the second and third periods, when the contestants go off the mat with one wrestler having the advantage and if the match is stopped because of injury or an illegal hold when one wrestler has the advantage. The official should assume a position in front of the wrestlers, facing the scoring table, when starting the match from referee's position or on the mat. Before starting the match, the referee should observe the following points for the man in the down position:

1. Are his hands, knees and feet parallel to each other?
2. Are his hands at least one foot in front of his knees?
3. Are his hands flat on the mat?
4. Is he sitting still?
5. Are his hands and knees spread too far apart?

The referee should observe the following points for the top man position:

1. Is his hand loose around the waist of the opponent?
2. Is his hand in the right position on his opponent's elbow?
3. Does his leg touch the opponent's leg?
4. Is his head in a legal position?
5. Is his knee outside of the parallel line of hand, knee or foot?[1]

When the referee is satisfied that the contestants have assumed their proper positions, he should raise his hand to indicate to the wrestlers and the timer that the match is ready to begin. The referee starts the match by sounding his whistle and bringing his arm down sharply. The referee should remain close to the contestants at all times to block illegal holds, to determine when the wrestlers go off the mat, to award points for takedowns, escapes, predicaments, near falls and falls. Most important, the referee should be in a position to prevent possible bodily injury to competitors.

1. Arnold W. Umbach and Warren R. Johnson, *Successful Wrestling* (Dubuque Ia.: Wm. C. Brown Company Publishers, 1972), p. 250.

FUNDAMENTAL SKILLS

Whistle

The whistle should be in good working order and available for immediate use. The whistle should be used only when necessary and forcefully when required to start and stop action.

Hand Signals and Awarding Points

Hand signals are important to convey, to the scoring table and the spectators, points scored, illegal holds and timeouts. Effective use of these signals should alleviate the need for lengthy discussions during the match. The referee should point to the wrestler who has gained the advantage and at the same time, holding his other hand high above his head, indicate the number of points to be awarded with his fingers extended upward. Verbal commands should accompany hand signals for clarification. This aids in keeping the wrestlers, scoring table and spectators informed as to what has happened when it happens. Communication of point awards is a must. Referees should not assume that the points are recorded. They should follow up by checking the scoreboard. If not, the match should be stopped and scoring should be rectified immediately.

BASIC PENALTIES AND RULINGS

Illegal Holds

Holds in this category include choke holds, holds that go against the normal limit of the joint and holds that are used for punishment. Special note should be given to the double wrist lock and chicken wing which becomes illegal when forced into a twisting hammerlock. Coaches should educate their wrestlers as to the cause and effect of these potentially dangerous holds.

TABLE 10.1

Illegal Holds

Hammerlock	Twisting hammerlock
Full nelson	Toe hold
Strangle hold	Front headlock without the arm
Finger holds	Body slam
Twisting knee lock	Potentially dangerous holds

Unsportsmanlike Conduct

The conduct of the contestants, coaches and spectators is the responsibility of the referee. Teammates, coaches and spectators should not be allowed to come within ten feet of the mat in order to eliminate the possibility of interference. If necessary, ejection from the premises may be required.

Unnecessary Roughness

Intentional striking, gouging, kicking, hair pulling, butting, elbowing or an intentional act which endangers life or limb should be penalized. A wrestler taking his opponent off the mat is responsible for his safe return to the mat. If he drops his opponent forcefully, he should be penalized.

Flagrant Misconduct

If in the opinion of the referee, the misconduct of a contestant, coach or spectator is of a flagrant nature, the penalty should be removal from the wrestling premises and a deduction of one team point.[2]

Scoring

The execution of maneuvers in an attempt to control and pin an opponent is the purpose of the wrestler. Successful execution of such maneuvers is the method for scoring individual points. The wrestler's performance in his individual match determines the number of team points scored.

TABLE 10.2

Individual Scoring

Takedown	2 points
Reversal	2 points
Escape	1 point
Predicament	2 points
Near fall	3 points
Time advantage	1 point
Penalties	1 point
	2 points
	disqualification

TABLE 10.3

Dual Meet Scoring

Fall, default, forfeit or disqualification	6 points
Decision	4 points (margin of more than 10)
	3 points (margin of less than 10)
Draw	2 points (for each team)

2. National Collegiate Athletic Association. *Wrestling Guide* (Phoenix: College Athletics Publishing Service, 1972), WR 34.

PROBLEM CALLS

Edge of the Mat Calls

If one wrestler has advantage position, the match should continue as long as the supporting parts of either wrestler remain within the boundary lines of the wrestling area. Wrestling should continue if a fall is imminent, as long as both shoulders of the defensive wrestler are within the boundary lines. Consistency in judgment on the part of the referee is imperative. Vacillation in this situation may destroy the confidence of the wrestlers and the coaches.

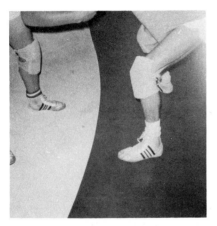

FIG. 10.4
Edge of the Mat Situation in Up-Position

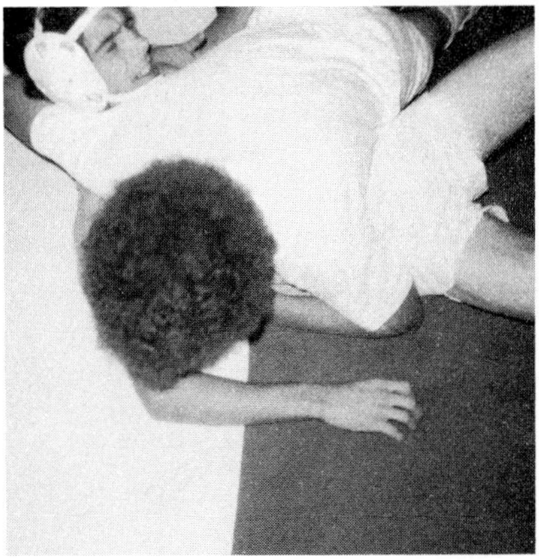

FIG. 10.5
Edge of the Mat Situation in Down-Position

Stalling

Stalling determinants should be clearly understood. Each wrestler should be working to improve his position or pin his opponent. The bottom man must make a legitimate attempt to gain control. Stalling penalties should be proceeded by a warning and strictly enforced. Consistency is again the key in this ruling.

Calling Falls, Near Falls and Predicaments

Novice officials are too anxious to award points for near falls and/or predicaments before the defensive wrestler escapes or time expires. Premature awarding of points could lead to a duplication in awards or two points for a predicament followed immediately by a three point award for a near fall. Each situation must be taken to its conclusion before the points are awarded. The predicament must be held for five seconds to be classified as a near fall. In order to call the fall, the referee should be down on the mat where he can see both scapulae in contact with the mat. When blocked out by entangled contestants, it is permissible to feel under the shoulders of the wrestler on your blind side to determine contact for the fall.

Interlocking Hands

The detection of which wrestler's hand is interlocked is difficult to determine. Too often a wrestler is penalized for interlocking hands when he actually has his opponent's hand. The referee should be positive before making this call. This situation is most prominent when the wrestlers are performing the standup.

OFFICIATING EVALUATED BY COACHES

What qualities do you appreciate in a wrestling official?

BOB SMITH—San Bernardino Valley College:

> The best officials that I have ever seen have been those who are inconspicuous during a match until action puts them on the scene.

FRED DAVIS—Brigham Young University:

> A referee that will talk to the wrestlers to prevent penalties and injuries.

WAYNE SKILL—Long Beach City College:

> The official that takes full authority after the meet is turned over to him.

FINN B. ERIKSEN—Waterloo Community Schools, NCAA Rules Committee, (1968-69):

> 1. Thorough knowledge of the rules and a wrestling background.
> 2. Consistency in enforcing rules.
> 3. Proper attire and neat appearance.
> 4. Prompt in arriving for a meet.
> 5. Proper signals given clearly and without hesitation.
> 6. Being in proper position on the mat especially when a fall is imminent.
> 7. Displaying alertness and keeping the match moving.
> 8. Courteous and forceful in enforcing the rules.
> 9. Being in control of the match at all times.
> 10. Emotional stability to meet unexpected situations.

DALE DEFFNER—Golden West College:

> 1. Hustle—was right on the situation to make the correct calls.
> 2. Knowledge of the rules—most up-to-date interpretations.
> 3. Was reserved in making "quick" decisions but was most efficient in making judgment quickly.
> 4. Kept contestants well informed.

What qualities do you dislike in a wrestling official?

DAVE McCUSKEY—University of Iowa:

> Calling stalling late in the match when it has occurred all during the match. If stalling is called when it occurs, the wrestler has a chance to make up the points.

GRADY PENINGER—Michigan State University:

> Giving a debatable decision for a wrestler because he had one called against him earlier in the match.

R. G. MACIAS—Mankato State:

> Slowness in calls and not being in position to make predicament calls—not physically fit to officiate.

ED PEERY—United States Naval Academy:

> Emotional involvement, being intimidated and a lack of interest.

Miscellaneous comment

DOUGLAS PARKER—Springfield College, NCAA Rules Committee (1968-69):

> The official must gain the respect of the wrestlers during his prematch inspection and talk. The outstanding official was a former wrestler, and is presently a coach with a good understanding of wrestling techniques, wrestling strategy, wrestling rules, and consequently, a very good interpretation of the rules. Because of his extensive experience, this official can demonstrate considerable confidence and remain calm during difficult calls.

OFFICIATING EVALUATED BY OFFICIALS

What is the most difficult situation to call in wrestling?

ORAN BREELAND—Fullerton College:

1. Edge of the mat calls.
2. Change of position or control as time expires.

JACK FERNANDEZ—Southern California Wrestling Coaches and Officials Association:

> Coaches teaching wrestlers to take advantage of the rules.

DEL TANNER—Morningside High School:

> Anticipating the next move to be in the proper position.

RON BRIDWELL—Millikan High School:

> Subjective calls which often bring disputes.

What is the most difficult phase of mechanics in officiating wrestling?

Gus Headington—Downey High School:

> Scoring points while continuing to observe the action.

Del Tanner—Morningside High School:

> See a pin in a cradle situation.

Oran Breeland—Fullerton College:

> Calling falls in fast changing situations (half nelson with bridging and twisting).

R. G. Nilson—California State College, Los Angeles:

> Falls when the shoulders are covered "front and back" and reversals on the edge of the mat.

Miscellaneous comments

Don Matson—Southern California Wrestling Officials Association.

> Most coaches think that they know the rules, but unfortunately they do not. Let the referee make the decisions. After meets, coaches should be *constructive* in their criticism of officials if they hope to have improved officiating.

H. R. Donald Cornett—Kern Wrestling Officials Association:

> I have officiated four of the major sports. I feel that I can frankly state that wrestling is the toughest sport of all to officiate without tremendous criticism. Every person in the audience, including the coaches, are officials in their own minds. Officials make mistakes. The mark of a good official is one who can admit or rectify a mistake. Wrestling is a highly emotional sport but one of the cleanest and finest in my opinion. It becomes much easier if a coach can develop the attitude that "the official is out there doing his job the way he sees it and I will abide by it."

Ken Ryman—1968 Olympic Training Camp Official:

> The outstanding wrestling official is consistent, knowledgeable and inconspicuous.

Bob Fischer—Southern California Wrestling Officials Association:

> Wrestling officiating is the most difficult because you are on your own to make all decisions.

MISCELLANEOUS CONSIDERATIONS

Weigh-Ins

Officials should be encouraged to arrive one hour before the match to conduct the weigh-ins. Otherwise the weigh-in must be administered by the host coach. This practice could result in the disqualification of a wrestler and determine the outcome of the meet. The coach should not be placed in such a vulnerable position.

In Case of Injury

A rest period is granted when a contestant is injured. The match should be resumed as if the contestants had gone out of bounds. If the injury is accidental, and the injured wrestler cannot continue, the opponent must receive team points equivalent to a fall. If the injury was the result of an illegal hold, the injured wrestler is declared the winner and scores the same number of team points won by a fall.

After the Match

At the conclusion of the match, the referee should be guided by the following principles:

1. The official should leave the scene of the contest immediately and go to the dressing room.
2. Any comments that the spectators make after the meet should be ignored.
3. He must never make any comments to the press or public concerning the match.
4. The official should never ask the coach to comment on how he worked the meet.
5. The official should not make alibis or pass the buck.
6. If the coach gets nasty, the official should keep silent but not work again for this type of coach.
7. If the official is asked to rate the school officials and contestants, he should wait a few days for a cooling off period.[3]

Influence of the Referee

A wrestler has only eight minutes to prove his superiority over his opponent. Therefore, the referee must dedicate himself to the orderly progress of each match. The referee can make the meet a success by following the spirit and absolute letter of the rules.

BIBLIOGRAPHY

National Collegiate Athletic Association. *Wrestling Guide*. Phoenix: Collegiate Athletic Publishing Service, 1972.
Umbach, Arnold W. and Warren R. Johnson. *Successful Wrestling*. Dubuque, Ia.: Wm. C. Brown Company Publishers, 1972.

3. Arnold W. Umbach and Warren R. Johnson, *Successful Wrestling* (Dubuque, Ia.: Wm. C. Brown Company Publishers, 1972), p. 264.

Index